Moments of Grace

true stories of those touched
by God's Grace

Moments of Grace
Copyright © 2008 Forever Books Publishing

All Rights Reserved. No part of this publication may be reproduced, stored in a retrieval system or transmitted in any form or by any means—electronic, mechanical, photocopy, recording or any other—except for brief quotations in printed reviews, without the prior permission of the author.

ISBN: 978-0-9783781-5-8

Scripture quotations marked "KJV" are taken from the *Holy Bible, King James Version*, Cambridge, 1769.

Scripture quotations marked "NIV" are taken from the *Holy Bible, New International Version*®. Copyright © 1973, 1978, 1984 International Bible Society. Used by permission of Zondervan Bible Publishers.

Scripture quotations marked "NASB" are taken from the *New American Standard Bible*®, Copyright © 1960, 1962, 1963, 1971, 1972, 1973, 1975, 1977, 1995 by The Lockman Foundation. Used by permission.

Scripture quotations marked "NKJV" are taken from the *Holy Bible, New King James Version* Copyright © 1982 by Thomas Nelson Inc. Used by permission. All rights reserved.

Scripture quotations marked "AKJV" are taken from the American King James version of the Bible, Michael Peter (Stone) Engelbrite, public domain, November 8, 1999.

Cover Design: Design Guys
Book Design: Andrew Mackay
Managing Editor: Beryl Henne
Printed in Canada
Published by

Forever Books

WINNIPEG MANITOBA
www.foreverbooks.ca

Dedicated to Gerry Wakeland,
Managing Director of CLASServices, Inc.

Thank you, Gerry, for your tireless example of unselfish commitment to excellence in everything you do for our Lord Jesus Christ.

- Carol Jones
- Reba Carolyn Rhyne
- Ruth Holland
- Anita Agers-Brooke
- Pam Morrison
- Allison Pittu
- Cheryl Dore
- Linda Mitchell
- Nancy Biffle
- Linda Gilden
- Susan Norris
- Ginger O'Neill
- Jen Taylor
- Rebecca Dowd
- Lesli Westfall
- Shawona Clark
- Linda Davis
- Caroline Coleman
- Daphne Delay
- Donna Savage
- Allison Johnson
- Doreen Hanna
- Kay Klebba
- Michal Parrott
- Ruby Heaton
- Michelle Bengtson
- Linda Savage Ditworth
- Penny Carlson
- Cynthia Zahm Siegfried
- Darin Jordan
- Carol Strutter
- Lesli Harvey
- Karen Porter
- Cheri Cowell
- Lee Warren
- Pamela Sonnemoser
- Gus Henne

Table of Contents

Introduction
  Linda Gilden 11
Season of Grace
  Nancy Davis Biffle 15
Grace on a Thursday
  Ally Johnson 21
To Everything There is a Season
  Carol Jones 25
True to His Word
  Susan Norris 29
Treasures of the Heart
  Linda B. Davis 35
A Modern Hannah's Prayers
  Reba Carolyn Rhyne 39
Grace at Three A.M.
  Linda Mitchell 45
Daunting Expectations
  Cheryl Dore 49

It's Time to Go
　Dr. Rebecca Dowden 53
My God, My God, Why Have I Forsaken You?
　Anita Agers-Brooks 57
How God Orchestrated My Life
　Ruth Holland 61
Sustaining Strength
　Dr. Michelle L. Bengtson 65
The Pony-Tailed Guy Goes to School
　Lawrence J. Clark 71
My Parting of the Red Sea
　Ruby Heaton 79
God's Waiting Room
　Ginger O'Neill 85
Souvenir
　Pam Morrison 91
Mirror, Mirror
　Daphne Delay 97
Living with the Giant
　Cynthia Zahm Siegfried 101
Hedge of Grace
　Shonda Savage Whitworth 107
That's the Cutest Kid
　Penny Carlson 113
"Take a Risk!"
　Jan Edith Taylor 119
The Perfect Mom for Cooper
　Kay Klebba 125
His Longings Linger
　Lesli Westfall 129
Talkin' to Jesus
　Michael S. Tarrant 135
Get Published Now 2008 Team 143

Introduction

My grace is sufficient for you, for my power is made perfect in weakness (2 Corinthians 12:9 NIV).

What do we love about our Heavenly Father? Is it the love He gives us when He wraps His arms around us and squeezes tightly? Is it that He gives us specific direction when we ask Him to guide us on our journeys through life? Is it because we are in awe of His great love for us in sending His Son to die for us? For each of us there is a different answer. But it probably has something to do with the unexpected moments when He gives you a glimpse of His grace, an undeserved touch of His hand.

We live in a fast-paced world, a world that rarely acknowledges its Creator. And yet He never gives up on us. Grace comes into our lives in many forms. It may come as an answer to a specific prayer. It may come in the midst of trials and suffering through a hug from a friend. The smile of a three-year-old may warm your heart in a way that could only be His grace.

But through whatever form God's grace comes into our lives, it is always enough. God's grace is sufficient for the moment. He will never send us just enough to get by. During those times when the world seems to be spinning around us and there is no way to get off for a moment of rest, God steps in and invites us to rest in Him. When there seems to be no solution to our problems, God's grace gently envelopes us and speaks to our hearts. When we feel like we can no longer stand under the pressure of hard times, God's power lifts us up and we experience His grace in a new way.

Grace is universal and available to all who ask for it. Grace is personal and touches each one of us as though God called our names in the midst of the crowd. The writers of this book know what it is like to search for answers, to yearn for Him. Their stories are very different for each author has struggled in his or her own way. But the message they share is the same. God is the One in control. His grace is sufficient. The authors of *Moments of Grace* are passionate about their stories and they want to share what God has done in their lives.

My prayer is that every reader of *Moments of Grace* will find affirmation of God's grace, courage to look for it in places least expected, and a desire to ask Him to meet every need. When we acknowledge our weakness and declare Him sufficient, God releases His power into our lives and we experiences moment after moment of His grace. Truly He is sufficient to meet our every need.

Linda Gilden
Director of Get Published Now!
Editorial Director, *Moments of Grace*

Let everyone be sure that he is doing his very best, for then he will have the personal satisfaction of a job well done, and won't need to compare himself with someone else. Each of us must bear some faults and burdens of his own. For none of us are perfect!

Galatians 6:4-5

Season of Grace

Nancy Davis Biffle

I lay beside my sleeping husband, my fingers tracing the small lump. I walked my fingers over and around it. No longer an insignificant bump, it now felt like a tiny twig, rough and uneven.

"It's nothing. Besides, it's tender. Cancerous lumps aren't supposed to hurt, right? I've had one biopsy and it was benign. I hate to make a big deal out of this." I regularly had this conversation with myself, knowing God listened. Sometimes I asked God directly, "Please don't let this be cancer. I don't have time for cancer."

The past four years had been grueling. I completed my Masters degree in counseling while teaching full-time with two children at home. Extra hours qualified me as a school counselor *and* a marriage and family therapist. That was behind me and so were the 2000 hours of clinical supervision. Nothing remained except taking the state exam to become a Licensed Professional Counselor (LPC). As an intern, I already had a part-time practice in a respected firm and a full-time job as an elementary school counselor. Daughter Regina was in seventh grade and our son Davis was a freshman in college. We had three grandchildren.

Additionally, I taught Bible studies, spoke at retreats, and sang in our church choir. There was no way I could work cancer into my schedule.

At the time, my gynecologist and I were seeing a lot of each other. I had cystic fibroid disease—an ever-increasing problem that required hormone therapy. When I decided to tell him about the lump, it was six months before my next scheduled mammogram.

Dr. Thomas wasn't overly concerned. "I'm almost sure it's benign, but I think I'll let Dr. Clark have a look at it. He's a fine surgeon and his wife has been fighting cancer for the last few years."

Dr. Clark examined the lump located on my rib cage at the base of my right breast. "I think Dr. Thomas was correct," he said. "It's probably benign but I want to take a biopsy and be sure. Let's schedule a date."

So far so good. Two doctors and I weren't worried. I wasn't so sure about my husband, George.

After "the procedure," George and I visited in the recovery room when Dr. Clark walked into the room. A single tear rolled down his cheek as he took my hand. "I'm so sorry. You have cancer," he said.

The news slammed into me like a sledgehammer. Inside I screamed. "No! What about my LPC exam?" Unbelievably, my first thought was I might not achieve my dream.

I heard Dr. Clark continue. "We will have to send the biopsy off to a lab to determine the type and stage of cancer. I tried to get it all, but I didn't. We'll schedule another surgery. It's still small so we can hope for a good prognosis. However, we won't know for about two weeks. In the meantime, you will have to stop your hormone replacement therapy."

"Uh-oh, George," I quipped. "You're in trouble now." George smiled weakly at my attempted humor.

Dr. Clark's smile and voice were gentle, "A sense of humor is a wonderful thing. It will get you through some tough times.

However, you must understand this is going to be equally hard for you and George. It's a serious matter."

He got through to me. This was real. This was frightening. Tears invaded my eyes. There were more instructions, but I was in a fog. Neither George nor I remember our conversation on the thirty-minute drive home. Exhausted, I headed straight for bed.

"I'll get you into bed but I *must* do this first." George fell to his knees beside me as I sat on the edge of the bed. He cried, "Oh, Lord, I love this woman. Please heal her. I can't imagine life without her. Give us strength to get through this frightening time. Please heal Nancy. Please. Please." His words faded into tears.

We clung to each other, wanting to believe this would have the outcome we desperately desired. George tucked me into bed as words like chemotherapy and mastectomy bounced around inside our heads. "I love you and always will," he said. "Inward beauty is far more important than outward appearance and you have more inward beauty than anyone I know." I knew a scarred or mutilated body wouldn't alter his love.

When I woke from drugged sleep, my daughter Robin called. She read to me from the chronological Bible I had given her. "*The* LORD *will sustain him upon his sickbed; In his illness, You restore him to health*" (Psalm 41:3 NASB).

"I believe that is for you, Mom. But the Lord also said that you are to "*be still and know that I am God*" (Psalm 46:10). It was unusual for Robin to tell me what God had in mind for me. I felt like Mary as I treasured her words and pondered them in my heart.

The most difficult part of the ordeal was the two-week wait for results.

Two weeks. At one time, I would have told you that two weeks is nothing—before we waited for answers to life and death questions. What kind of cancer did I have? What treatment would I endure? Would I have to have a mastectomy? God's grace is greater than all my questions.

Two weeks. Time to contemplate death, the value of life and love. George and I became truly one. When I worried, he was strong enough for both of us. When he was sad, my optimism overflowed into his heart. Family and friends sent food, cards, and Bible verses. They visited and prayed—grace personified.

Two weeks. Time to be still before God. I entered a sort of never-never land when sleep ignored the clock, when I relied on the Comforter as never before. One night He woke me at 4:30 a.m. I lay in bed thinking about prayer and possible answers—yes, no, wait. I "think" in God's presence. I knew He was listening and helping me with truth. He can't lie. I trusted my Father's commitment to answer if I called. Thoughts of love and death swirled around in my head, keeping me from sleep.

I slipped out of bed and headed for the computer to record my thoughts and prayer. Like the poet in Psalm 104—I alternated between speaking about God and speaking to Him.

"Father, I ask to be healed because I have a thirteen-year-old daughter and a twenty-year-old son who need their mother to help them plan a wedding someday. George needs someone to hold his hand and grow old with him. I have children and grandchildren who need to hear how God taught this aging woman to love and trust and even to obey. I am needed. I ask on behalf of all those I love. Please God, heal me!"

For over an hour, beliefs about God's character and promises wrestled with agonizing thoughts over treatments and outcome. I remembered my initial response to the diagnosis.

"Lord, I lay aside my dreams of a career in counseling and put my healing and our relationship above all other things. I'll direct what energy You give first to You and then to my family. If there is energy left, it will go to completing my Licensed Professional Counselor."

My body told me it was late—or early.

"Even now, I savor this time we've had together. It is 7:00 a.m. and this time has magically disappeared. The fellowship has been sweet and I'm ready to rest. Thank You that tomorrow, rather today, is Labor Day and I have the opportunity to rest. I praise You for providing for my every need. Help me recognize Your provision.

"I also thank You for the card of encouragement that came today. It personalized Psalm 91: 14-16: 'Because she has loved Me, therefore I will deliver her; I will set her securely on high, because she has known My name. She will call upon Me, and I will answer her; I will be with her in trouble; I will rescue her and honor her. With a long life I will satisfy her and let her see My salvation.' "

How amazing and precious that my friend thought that verse applied to me, nevertheless I inhaled it as a precious life-breath.

"My love is feeble in comparison to Yours. I'm grateful that You accept my childlike love. I confess it isn't always whole-hearted, but with Your help, I pray it will become so.

"I thank You for my precious husband, my family, and friends who demonstrate Your love in beautiful ways. I am truly blessed and there is no one happier than I am."

Eleven years later, that remains true.

NANCY DAVIS BIFFLE (wordsoflife.nb.@sbcglobal.net) is a speaker and retreat leader through Words of Life Ministries. Nancy's careers include marriage and family therapist, school counselor, and special needs teacher. She delights in her husband, children, stepchildren, and grandchildren. She and her husband volunteer in Costa Rica where their daughter lives as a missionary.

Grace on a Thursday

Ally Johnson

When we feel unlovely we want to hide because we can't imagine anyone could love us in those moments. Let's face it—we all have those moments, and that's usually when God speaks the loudest.

My Grammie was one of the loveliest women I have ever known, but one Thanksgiving she didn't think so. Our tradition was to dress up in our Sunday best, dine at two and go to the movies. We all knew with Grammie being sick there would be no movie this year. Released from the hospital two days earlier, we were just happy she could be with us for the holiday. But now another storm was brewing.

"Mom!" My sister ran into the kitchen. "Grammie says she's not coming to dinner. She says she doesn't have anything to wear, her hair isn't done and she is not about to come to dinner in her pajamas and robe." Laura's green eyes pleaded with Mom. "What are we going to do? We can't leave her in her room all alone ... not on Thanksgiving." Nervous knots formed in my belly as I wondered what would happen.

A few days earlier I had taken a trip to the hospital. My mind hadn't comprehended the seriousness of Grammie's condition until I stood in the doorway of her room and was struck by her frailty. I paused for a moment taking in the image of my sweet Grammie lying in that hospital bed looking like a small child. Without the benefit of going to the salon, her normally jet black hair had turned gray. Her milky white complexion had grown sallow and pale. Broken blood vessels from her IV etched the skin of her once smooth hand.

The contrast to her usual self was startling. Throughout my childhood, Grammie had come over for dinner on a Thursday after her weekly hair and nail appointment. Smelling of Estee Lauder perfume, she would sink into the sofa and beckon to me with her beautiful hands. I loved sitting next to her, and my heart would sing at the invitation to be near her. I breathed her in while listening to her soft, gentle voice tell me about the events of her day, and then she would ask me about mine. Her hands stroked my back or played with my hair. She made me feel safe and loved. But in the past few years the allure of college and my social life had kept me from spending Thursdays with her. And now she was in the hospital.

I moved closer to her hospital bed and picked up her IV-pierced hand. She smiled at me and asked me about my day. It felt just like our old Thursday afternoons, only we were conversing over the starched white sheets of her hospital bed, with the scent of antiseptic lingering in the air. She couldn't reach out and stroke my back anymore, but I could curl up beside her and stroke her hair and smell her sweet perfume. Even in the hospital she still smelled like flowers. I cradled her hand in mine while her words curled around my heart. She loved me unconditionally and in that moment I saw Jesus. Like Christ, she gave to me even though I hadn't made her a priority over the past few years.

The hospital released her for Thanksgiving and as the scent of roasting turkey and pumpkin pie filled the air, my sister and I watched our mother, wondering what to do. Mom told us not to worry while she placed an apple pie into the oven. I could see her shoulders quietly shake as she tried to hide her emotion from us.

"Mom, what if I fix her hair and put a little makeup on her," Laura said. "I think that might help her feel better."

"Yes, I think that's a great idea, but let's do more than that." She stirred the gravy and then a smile broke through the clouds that had covered her face. "I know ... let's wear our bathrobes to the table. We can surprise her!" Pausing for a moment to let the idea sink in she continued, "We can wear our normal clothes underneath and each of us can come to the table in our robes. That way she will know that she fits right in. What do you think?" Her face shone with excitement, and I knew we had our answer.

Laura nodded her head in agreement. "I'll go tell her that we aren't taking no for an answer and insist that she let me fix her hair. Even though we all think she's beautiful without being fixed up, knowing Grammie there isn't going to be any other way to convince her."

We thought we would surprise her so we didn't tell Grammie of our plan. After a "We're not taking no for an answer" conversation with my mother, Grammie finally let my sister Laura fix her hair and apply a little color to her cheeks.

I will never forget how excited I felt when I stood next to my chair at the dining room table. I looked around the table at my family. We were attired in our Sunday best, our bathrobes draped over our shoulders. My little brother even had on his slippers and was grinning from ear to ear. We barely contained ourselves with the excitement of our secret and hoped that Grammie would feel a part of our family as she had on so many other Thursday afternoons.

Dad wheeled her into the dining room, her normally robust frame wilting in the wheelchair. We stood quietly at the table until she looked up. When she did, we shouted "Surprise!" Her face went from pale gray to a soft blush, and a giant smile engulfed her face. She giggled my favorite giggle and for a moment she was my joyful, adoring Grammie again.

Tears of relief rolled down my cheeks, she was with us again, and we were all overjoyed! Conversation bubbled across the table as we shared our Thanksgiving meal. I believe we were all thankful that our family was complete. It would not have been the same without our Grammie.

Grammie died two days later. For her funeral we dressed once again in our Sunday best. I wished we could have worn our robes again. It seemed appropriate that in one of her final moments here on earth Grammie was more beautiful to me than ever, without the earthly adornments of hair color and makeup. Grace is God's way of pouring out His love upon us regardless of our clothing, whether we feel lovely or not. To Him we are always lovely, a fragrant aroma and a blessing. He accepts us, offers us grace when we don't deserve it and puts on our humanity out of love, every single day of the week.

ALLY JOHNSON is a certified Life Coach, former third grade teacher and graduate of the Wise Counsel Training Program. She is currently building a ministry for women called "ResurrectedGirl" and has a website and blog. Ally lives in San Antonio, Texas with her husband Grant and her two children, Zachary and Kayla. www.resurrectedgirl.com

To Everything There is a Season

Carol Jones

I awoke early one spring morning to hear birds singing outside my window. Their song, beautiful and melodic, was music to soothe any savage beast. I lay in bed, eyes closed, drinking in what would without doubt be a beautiful day. The bird's song made me feel peaceful and secure inside. I thought, "Oh my. The birds are singing, the sun is shining, and it's going to be a beautiful day." I lay there feeling good, imagining what the day would be like: my children and I playing out back in the woods, or walking along the bike path. There is something very calming about a sunny day in the spring after a cold, dark winter.

I opened my eyes, ready to enjoy this perfect day. To say I was shocked at what I saw would be an understatement. To my surprise, the sun was not shining. It was very dark and raining on top of that. I could not believe my eyes. I felt betrayed. How could the birds sing such a beautiful song? How could they be so cheerful through this rain?

"What?" I yelled in amazement, "The birds lied." I couldn't believe birds were capable of deception. My heart was let down. How could the birds fool me with such deliberate intention?

My disappointment at losing my beautiful day must have awakened my husband. He turned towards me looking puzzled. "What are you talking about?" he yawned as he sat up in bed. How could he have slept through the deceit? "The birds were singing so beautifully," I said. "I thought today was going to be warm and sunny. Instead, it looks dark and cold!"

"They didn't lie," he said. "For them it is a sunny day and a day worth singing about. They sing because they know that the cold, the rain, and darkness holds no power over them. They sing, loud with excitement, because it's their season. In spite of the weather, their winter is past, spring is here, they've made their flight from the south and it's their season."

What a profound thought! I don't think to this day he knows the great impact that one statement had on me! God permitted the birds to sing at my window just to get a message to me. He knew a storm was brewing in my life, and in a few months I would need that little incident to help me through a trying time. The Bible says *"Before they call I will answer"* (Isaiah 65:24 KJV). Before I even knew to what extent I was going to need Him, God had already answered.

Months after the incident with the birds, I was thrown into the midst of the fiery furnace. This testing of my faith shook me to the core of my being.

My husband committed adultery.

I was in total disbelief. Like most women, I never thought it would happen to me. He never appeared to be the type of man who would be unfaithful. The Bible tells us not to think of any man more highly than we ought. Maybe I thought too much of him.

I kept hoping it was a bad dream. I kept waiting to wake up, or for him to say it was a joke. But it was not a dream, and he was not joking. He had committed adultery and a week later I came home to find him gone. I had three young children at the time, and the youngest was often sick. At least once a month, our son was in the emergency room, and sometimes the hospital. Yet not one time did I wonder what I was going to do. I was in shock and disbelief, but somewhere down inside there was a calming peace. This inner tranquility was unexplainable, and somehow I knew things were going to work out alright.

My husband didn't want to be responsible for any of my household expenses. The only debt he paid was the mortgage since his name was on the deed. He turned off the electricity, the gas, and the water. He didn't appear to care how his wife and three children were going to make it.

Somehow Satan had tricked him into believing that the grass was greener on the other side and he was blinded by the color. He didn't realize that his grass would have been just as green, if he'd only taken the time to water it.

Those days after he left were trying, but God proved faithful in every circumstance. I didn't know how I was going to come through the trial, but I felt strong—encouraged by the power of God. I knew he was right there with me. I knew that the other side of what I was going through would make me better than I had been. Through God's eyes, I saw better times ahead.

Some days seemed bleak, like the day of the birds. The sun didn't shine, and I felt I was in a storm. God was there guiding me through it all. He held my hand and led the way. So like the birds, I sang. I sang in the most beautiful voice. Winter was over, spring was here, I had flown in from the south, and it was my season. I sang loud and clear like the birds.

Friends who knew what was going on didn't understand how I could be so happy. They thought I should be upset. They offered suggestions about what I should do, but the very grace of God had me floating on air, and because of that grace I could sail through anything. It was my season. It was my season to learn more about God. It was my season to see the word and power of God in action. It was my season to grow in faith. It didn't matter that some did not understand.

Whatever came my way, grace and peace came also. God had prepared a way out. This testing of my faith was to bring me closer to God and help me grow into the person he wanted me to become. It was my season. There was no need for me to doubt. There was no need for me to be anxious. The word of God teaches us to *"be anxious for nothing,"* (Philippians 4:6, NASB).

Because of the lesson of the singing birds, I was able to be at peace. There was no need to be alarmed. I, too, was able to sing in the midst of my storm.

Jeremiah 33:3 (AKJV), says, *"Call unto me, and I will answer and show you great and mighty things, which you know not."* God showed me great things. Because of the lesson of the singing birds, I can say like David, *"It was good that I was afflicted."* I got to know God. I got to see God in His glory. Because of the lesson of the singing birds, I understood and felt the peace of God, knowing that because I am engraved on the palm of His hand, and by His grace, I can make it through whatever comes my way. I can make it, because as long as I am a child of God, it is my season.

That was seventeen years ago. We have now been married twenty-eight years. My husband repented, and God has restored our marriage. God has blessed us to raise three wonderful children. He healed our son's illness and my husband has excelled in his business. I have grown in the faith and wisdom of God, and I have learned to trust God, despite the circumstances. I know that God will do what he said he will do. He is true to his Word.

CAROL JONES lives with her husband of twenty-eight years, her son and her daughter's cat. She speaks at women's retreats and mentors young women on self-esteem. She inspires hope in others and encourages faith in Jesus Christ. Carol is a CLASS graduate, a Certified Personality Trainer and helps children with special needs. She would love to hear from you at gr8hope4u@aol.com.

True to His Word

Susan Norris

My eyes popped open at 4:30 a.m. There was no hope of sleep. Steve, my younger brother, lay in a hospital four and a half hours away in Charlotte, and the doctors were baffled. I jumped in the shower, dressed, grabbed my suitcase and hit the road before daylight. Whether Steve needed me to be there or not, I needed to be there.

I arrived at University Hospital and hurried to his room. I walked in to see my parents' concerned faces and my thirty-one-year old brother in bed looking eight months pregnant. Steve trains for triathlons and personifies excellent health. How could he be here?

My parents brought me up to speed. After three days of tests and treatment for a bowel blockage, we should have seen some progress. I could tell from the look on Steve's face, he was skeptical. I questioned the nurse.

Steve joked, "My sister is here now. She'll pester you to death with questions." Little did we know that pestering the staff would be necessary to keep him alive.

The day crawled like cold molasses.

When the doctor arrived, Steve said, "If all I have to do is wait around for something to pass through my system, I can do that at home."

Dr. Albright said, "I might consider discharging you, but I want to run one more test."

The results of the test changed Dr. Albright's plan. "You have appendicitis and it appears your appendix ruptured since you've been here. We need to get a surgeon in there and clean things up. It's a routine procedure and once it's done, you'll be back to normal."

The surgery took place without any surprises. A young nurse dressed in green scrubs announced, "Steve is in recovery and will be in his room soon."

With that good news, my father drove ninety miles back home to take care of things at work and return the next day with fresh clothes.

The minute Steve returned to his room, Mom and I knew all was not well. His heart rate escalated and his body temperature skyrocketed.

At the nurses' station, I pulled the nurse aside. "I don't want to alarm my mom, but I know Steve's heart rate as an athlete is normal low and it's now 168. And besides that, his temperature isn't coming down. Something's wrong."

She called the doctor to share our concerns. "The doctor ordered no changes. I will pack him in ice. Maybe we'll bring his temperature down."

"I'm cold. Can you get me another blanket?" Steve asked.

We covered him with a blanket but his body was hot to the touch. We placed an icy washcloth on his forehead and it warmed on the spot. Nothing worked. His heart rate escalated higher and higher and his temperature remained high.

I felt helpless. Something had to change. I confronted the nurse. "My brother will not die because of bad health care. Do something!"

She called the doctor. She mouthed to me, "No change in the

orders."

Exasperated, the nurse yelled into the phone, "He will not die on my watch." She slammed the phone down, turned to face me with fear in her eyes and said, "Let's go!"

"We're taking you to ICU," the nurse said. An orderly assisted with the IV pole; however, once the nurse began pushing Steve down the hall, the orderly lagged behind.

"I've got it," I said as I took the pole from the orderly and yelled, "Go!"

We ran down the hall like a scene from ER. At the elevator, she rammed the bed inside, pushed the up button, willed the elevator to move us upstairs.

It went down.

Her eyes flew to mine and I saw raw fear. When the doors opened, she screamed, "We're full!" and pushed the button to take us back up. Somewhere between the lobby and the ICU floor, Steve's breathing labored. She frantically pumped the compression bag over his mouth to make him breathe. No one said a word. In my mind I prayed, "Lord, help him!"

When the elevator doors opened, she shoved his bed and took off. The doctors and nurses came through the ICU doors and met us in the hall.

"We'll take it from here."

The doors closed.

"God, please let him live."

Mom and I spent the night in the waiting room sleeping in chairs and on the floor. We didn't dare leave. We had to know.

He stabilized and the doctor called us together. "Steve still has infection in his body. There's an abscess and it has to come out. This means more surgery."

Dad arrived early next morning and joined us in the ICU. Steve was in surgery and we waited with more questions. The surgery went well and he stabilized in ICU. It had been a long day. Steve needed to sleep and so did we. We left our phone numbers with the nurse and checked into a hotel.

Mom and Dad paced and ate like robots. I slammed things around the room. It's absurd! Steve was healthy?

We crawled into bed, turned the light out, and the telephone rang.

The ICU nurse said, "The pulmonary specialist is here to evaluate Steve's condition and thinks it would be best to put him on life support so he can stop fighting so hard to breathe and allow his body to focus on healing. Steve wants you to come up to the hospital." He refused treatment without talking with us first.

We met with the doctor in Steve's room. He explained how they would induce a coma and put Steve on life support so he could heal. Steve looked at me with frightened eyes and said, "What would you do?"

"By doing this," I said, "you have a chance to heal. Without it, your body will use all of its energy to breathe. It seems obvious what you need to do."

Steve looked away with tears in his eyes and agreed.

I prayed with him, "Lord, we're scared. We have no idea how to battle this. We are trusting in you. Please guide the doctor's hands and give them wisdom and discernment. Give Steve your peace, Lord, and comfort us all. In your Son's precious name, Amen."

Mom and Dad spent time with Steve, then exited the room so the doctors could perform the procedure. It was as if we plunged into the dark with no clue of what waited around the next bend. We had no idea Steve would spend five weeks on the ventilator, most of those in a medically-induced coma.

I drove home Monday night and begged God to spare my brother's life. "Steve is my baby brother. He has his whole life ahead of him. This can't be happening. Please let him live."

I felt a warm sensation come over me as if the Lord pulled me in his lap and wrapped his arms around me in a warm embrace—

the peace that surpasses all understanding. I am certain I heard God tell me Steve would live. I clung to that promise.

I felt pulled in two directions. I had a husband and two young children who needed me in Marietta and a brother fighting for his life in Charlotte. I divided my week between the two. Tuesday through Thursday I stayed home with my family. Friday through Monday I battled for Steve's life in Charlotte.

We sat with Steve in shifts so he was never alone. During the course of the weekend, friends, family, and church members made the drive to the hospital to show their support. Friends from Georgia couldn't make the drive, but sent cards and letters we taped around Steve's room. Over 200 Scriptures and words of encouragement covered the walls of his room.

When the doctors brought Steve out of the coma, he saw the reminders of hope surrounding him on the wall.

He walked from the hospital forty days after he entered it. He looked weak and feeble, but he was alive. He would battle back. He would do more than survive; he was determined he would thrive.

Our older brother, David, told him,

"All great people have a story to tell. You have your story; now go do something great."

With help from his professors, Steve graduated six months later. He packed everything and moved across the country to attended graduate school at the University of Colorado at Boulder.

While in graduate school, he met his future business partner. After graduation, they started their own design/build company, Steve's dream job of building homes and neighborhoods. A few years later, he met and married the love of his life, had a beautiful daughter and another baby on the way. In November of 2007, Steve completed the Ironman race he trained for since 1999. God was faithful to His promise. Steve is alive today and is blessed abundantly. John 10:10 (NIV) says,

"*The thief comes only to steal, and kill, and destroy; I came that they might have life, and might have it abundantly.*" The Lord is true to his Word.

Susan Norris is a former elementary school teacher whose passion is to teach the power of prayer and God's Word. She is a Bible teacher, motivational speaker, and author. She lives in Marietta, Georgia, with her husband, Mark, and her children, Sam and Laura.

Treasures of the Heart

Linda B. Davis

"Mom, it's me."

In the silent space between two heartbeats, the past returned without mercy.

"That you, Lane?" My whispered words trembled.

"Yes. I need to talk."

"Come on over," I answered, stunned to hear my son's voice after so many years.

"Thanks. Be there in thirty minutes."

I placed the telephone in its cradle, but my hand lingered as if holding a lifeline. Bending uncertain knees, I prayed, "Let this be the day he comes home to you, Lord."

I settled into the old rocker that soothed Lane's colic twenty years before. *This old thing's as marked by the years as I am*, I thought.

Leaning back, I remembered the past. We lived in several houses when Lane was a boy, but images of the last house overwhelmed the others. Revelations of adultery unfolded within its walls. Accusations and counter-accusations rose to the ceiling and pierced our hearts. Rather than repent, Lane's dad attacked like a cornered badger. "If you hurt my Army career, you'll regret it," he promised me. "Remember I have Lane's mind in my hands. I will turn him against you if you make me." I pictured empty rooms filled with verbal and emotional abuse, haunted spaces where Lane's home crumbled and his tender heart broke.

Separation and divorce followed. Our address changed, but the pain continued. In coming years, Lane's father heaped more and more abuse on him. The childhood stories I'd told Lane about his heavenly Father's love faded into oblivion as Lane searched for ways to relieve the pain his earthly father inflicted. In desperation, Lane lashed out at me to please his dad.

I held ten years of memories in my lap while the hands of the clock counted seconds, eighteen hundred of them.

When the doorbell rang, I jumped. *Steady my heart, Lord*, I prayed as I opened the door. One glimpse of my son, and my arms rose to enfold him. "Welcome home, Son," I said as my hands and eyes went to his face and rested there. With a mother's love, I took in every line on his sun-baked face.

Lane glanced around. "The house smells the way I remember it—like supper on the stove. I'm home, Mom. I'm home."

I could only nod as I reached for his coat. I noticed it carried his warmth. *When did my boy grow into clothes the size of his dad's?* I shook my head in wonder.

"Mom," Lane stammered as he took my hand, "sit down. I have something to say. Can't wait any longer." Lane took his place on the embroidered ottoman, and I sat in the rocker. He hung his head, his elbows on his knees. When Lane looked at me, his eyes brimmed with sorrow. He opened his mouth but could not speak. He lowered his head into his hands, and his shoulders shook.

"What's on your mind, Son?"

Lane shook his head and sobbed. A wellspring fuller and stronger than any spring in Comal County overcame my work-roughened son. Tears from a heart of sorrow and regret flowed freely into his hands. They crept down his face and onto his shirt. *I never knew eyes could make so many tears*, I thought. *Is there no end? Why, his shirt's soaked. Like the woman washing the feet of Jesus with her tears.*

Then Lane knelt by me. His arms encircled me, and still he sobbed. "I'm sorry, Mom," he mumbled into my shoulder. "I'm sorry for all I've done. Sorry for hurting you. I've been a horrible son. Can't ever make it up to you. I don't expect you to forgive me. I've done too much. Just wanted to see you again … to tell you I'm sorry."

By then, I was on my knees as well. "Oh, Lane," I replied as I held him, "you're my boy. You've done nothing that could quench my love. You never could."

Lane protested. "No, Mom, I've taken too much. I took your money and squandered it. Took your sterling silver—your family heirloom—for heaven's sake. Took your love and trampled it. And for what? To please a father who doesn't know what love is."

"I knew what was behind it, Lane," I replied. "It was your hurt talking, not your heart. You didn't know what to do with all that pain."

Returning to the ottoman, Lane wiped his eyes with the back of his hand. "How could I have turned on you, Mom? You've done nothing but love me. Dad set me on a pathway of bitterness. I was just a boy, but he filled me with anger. How could a man do that to his own boy?"

"The human heart's capable of the vilest sort of wickedness, Son. It's a product of sin. God gives us the freedom to open our hearts to good or evil. Some choose evil. At times, I've chosen to do wrong. Lord knows, I failed your dad time and time again. I've made many a choice for wrong while calling myself a Christian. But the human heart can choose to love as well. Love comes from God." I pointed to a framed embroidery of 1 John 4:8. "God *is* love, in fact."

Lane wiped his face with the kitchen towel I wore over my

shoulder. His elbows on his knees, he hung his head defeated. "Too much, Mom. I've done too much."

I cradled Lane's face in my hands and replied, "Son, God used the loss of my marriage, my home, and my worldly goods to show me my true treasure is Jesus. In the light of His mercy and grace, worldly treasures dimmed. I realized Matthew 6:21 says my heart always follows my treasure. When I placed you on one side of a scale and my silver on the other, I chose you, my heart's treasure. I always will."

In silence, Lane embraced me with tear-stained eyes.

"Let's put the past to rest," I offered.

"How, Mom? How can I?"

"Hand it to Jesus. He'll know what to do with it. He's changed your heart already. That's why you're here."

"How do I start over?"

"Go to Him like you came to me, Son. You can trust Him, so tell Him what's in your heart. Pray for your dad, too. He needs God, that's for sure. Open your heart to God's grace, Lane. Joel 2:25 says that when God's people repent, He restores what the locusts have eaten. He'll do that for you too, Son. He'll give you a future built on Jesus, the Solid Rock."

Lane took my hand and helped me from the rocker to the floor. With a sudden, soft gasp, he said, "Mom, the weight's lifting. I can breathe again." He brought his hands to his chest and began to pray.

What Lane had held, he released. What I had lost, I found. I leaned my head on my boy, smiling.

LINDA B. DAVIS, a forty-year veteran of special education, is a freelance writer working on her first novel. She has written for LIVE magazine, It's Too Soon to Say Goodbye: The Heartbreak of Suicide (New Hope Publishers, 2009), and a local newspaper. Linda and her husband live in Texas where they dote on six grandchildren.

A Modern Hannah's Prayers

Reba Carolyn Rhyne

The effectual fervent prayer of a righteous man availeth much (James 5:16 KJV).

The noises coming from the barn weren't understandable, except for the loud cry, "Oh, God!" They were the sounds of a young man, a modern Jacob, wrestling with His Heavenly Father. He may have been praying, preaching, or shouting questions at the Father. The agony in his voice pierced the heart of anyone who heard. What was going on? His mother who stood at the open kitchen window felt his anguish, but this time she couldn't make the decision for him. He must decide alone. One thing his mother knew, the wrong decision would make him a miserable man.

For years his mother, a contemporary Hannah, had prayed for a minister among her three sons. This son was the anointed one. She knew it! He was the deep thinker, the serious child, for whom she prayed.

Hearing the faraway commotion coming through the kitchen window where she stood washing the dishes immediately prompted her to pray. The harder she prayed the more vigorously she scrubbed the dishes, clattering them against each other. Some of the time she spoke audibly, but most of the time her lips moved silently. At times, tears flowed down her cheeks, splashing into the soapy dishwater. There were no eloquent words, just simple mountain talk from a woman who loved God and who possessed tremendous faith in Him.

As a young child, the sound of my beloved uncle's voice disturbed and distressed me. I wanted to rush into the house and question my grandmother. Instead, I watched as she stepped into her closet with the God she worshipped and to whom she prayed. Her beloved son was struggling against God and a life-changing decision. Although my grandmother was washing the dinner dishes, she was connected, mind latched onto her prayer link to heaven. There was no special key or secret password to enter the Holy of Holies. She did not need an earthly man or machine to connect. She only needed Christ to whisper her praises and petitions into the Father's ear. God's omni-hearing understood her silent words.

The strange noises from the barn ceased. Timidly, I approached her asking why my uncle was so upset.

"Don't worry about it," she said. "He's struggling through a problem." She didn't explain this difficulty or why she prayed so fervently.

His struggle continued for many days, even months until he became physically sick. As he lay in bed, sick with a fever, chills, and shaking violently, his mother hovered anxiously over him, remembering another time. Desperate, she called their minister.

The minister, a senior pastor, immediately understood the situation and spoke the exact words the young man needed. As he left the house, he whispered to the mother, "He'll be alright now." Unable to continue his struggle any longer against his Heavenly Father, my uncle, totally broken, answered, "Yes." Later, he emerged from the room and fell into his mother's embrace.

A Modern Hannah's Prayers

The three important things my grandmother taught me about prayer were to discover God's grace in attitude, belief, and benefit:

God's grace involves attitude. Who among us is righteous? Who deserves to fill God's ear with problems? God made a way for Christ-followers to approach Him through His death on the cross. Surely we can honor Him, emptying our mind of everything but His glorious presence in our thoughts. Even though the noise of battle swirls around us, we close the closet door and focus on Him. He is the sovereign ruler of the universe and our hearts. His position demands this attitude. My uncle's prayer closet was the drafty barn. My grandmother's her comfortable kitchen. Whatever or wherever we pray, personal passionate prayer will be attended to and answered. Our verse promises that.

God's grace requires belief. Our words are futile, clamoring or confused utterances, if we don't believe Jesus' words. He said,

> *Ask, and it shall be given you ... for everyone who asketh receiveth. Whatsoever ye ask in prayer, believing, ye shall receive. When thou prayest, enter into thy closet, and when thou hast shut thy door, pray ... thy Father which seeth in secret shall reward thee openly ... your Father knoweth what things ye have need of, before ye ask...* (Matthew 7:7-8, 21:22, 6:6-8).

On entering her closet, my grandmother prayed expecting to receive an answer to her prayer. Years before, during the loss of a son, age sixteen, and daughter, age fourteen, within a month of each other, the power of prayer strengthened her. She needed His strength urgently and God attended her broken heart.

Why would Jesus ask us to pray if He already knows what we want and need? Because our Father doesn't rush in and fulfill needs automatically; He needs and wants our permission. Grandmother's okay released Him to complete her prayer with

His undeserved favor. Ask first, and then He can and will proceed with His perfect knowledge. How long should Christ-followers pray? Saint Francis of Sales (1567-1622) states, "Every Christian needs a half hour of prayer each day, except when he is busy and then he needs an hour." Most importantly, we trust God will answer the need put before Him. And when the answer comes, we must be happy with the results.

God's grace becomes a benefit. The precious benefit of prayer is laying our burdens at His feet and coming away with square shoulders, our load lightened. During the day, my grandmother worked cheerfully, knowing the Father addressed her problems with perfect knowledge. We shouldn't wait until the roof caves in, as one great American, Abraham Lincoln, sometimes did, "I have been driven many times to my knees by the overwhelming conviction that I had nowhere else to go." My grandmother, on the other hand, prayed in advance.

Her prayers were answered when her son became a minister. Her legacy includes three other children who became Christ-followers. Four grandchildren became ministers and all the others are believers. This legacy is continuing into the third generation because a modern Hannah prayed.

REBA CAROLYN RHYNE is a consultant to the marine industry. She refers to her work in Missouri and Texas as her "turtle life." When she travels, her home goes with her. Living in the foothills of the Smoky Mountains, she hikes and visits with her family. She enjoys three church families but is a member of East Maryville Baptist.

Do not worry about what you are going to say or how you will say it; when the time comes, you will be given what you will say. For the words you will speak will not be yours; they will come form the Spirit of your Father speaking through you.

Matthew 10:19-20

Grace at Three A.M.

Linda Mitchell

Why did I choose to live in a dark corner of Mississippi instead of a bright, wear-your-shades-everyday state? I wondered at the end of this grey winter day. Normally the rain makes for good snoozing and when combined with the comforting snoring sounds coming from my husband, usually guarantees sleep.

But not tonight. My mind wanders to our boys. The oldest, living his dream life on a sailboat on another continent, spends much of his life diving with the sharks. The youngest lives in an athletic dorm on a nearby campus where a coach now makes certain he is tucked in for the night. Physical separation has no effect on their permanent dwelling places in my heart. Each has homesteaded there, creating a space uniquely his own, complete with accessories, add-ons, and sentimental treasures packed away but not forgotten.

Talking to God proves much more effective than counting sheep. "Dear Father," I pray, "Being a mom is a blessing, but the guy who said it wasn't for cowards was right. It competes with the highest roller coaster for chills and thrills. Thank you for answering the prayer I've breathed over them since they were babies and allowing them to grow as Jesus did, in wisdom, in stature, and in favor with God and people. Just because they're not there yet, doesn't mean they won't arrive at some point. Both are still works in progress. O Father, help them to make wise choices, and even when they make foolish ones—and I know they will, I still do—please keep them safe. They need a fleet of guardian angels to watch over them.

Way better than counting sheep. The peace I experience from giving God my worries allows me to drift off to sleep.

The shrill, incessant ringing awakes me. After a few bangs on the snooze button, I see that the display reads 3 A.M. and the noise comes from the telephone not the alarm.

"Hello," I mumble, sitting on the side of the bed.

"This is the county sheriff. Do you have a son named Torrey Mitchell?"

"Yes, what's wrong? Is he alright?" I barely have enough breath to ask.

"We found his truck. Looks like he lost control in a curve and flipped it."

I feel the solid support of my husband's arm around me. I know I should say something but can't form the words. "O God, please."

The sheriff says, "He's not in the truck; we're searching the area. Do you know where he might go?"

My husband takes the phone, "We'll be right there."

I don't imagine my son lying in a ditch, hurting, rain washing away the blood. Instead, I see him when the doctor placed him in my arms.

"Hello, so good to finally meet you," I say, carefully counting each tiny finger and toe. I marvel at his steady heartbeat, his miniature features so perfectly formed. Such a tiny miracle covered in soft new skin that will stretch and grow to one day wrap the body of a man. O God, this must be how you love me, so fiercely and protectively—close in your embrace.

"God, I know you love Torrey. You must have laughed when the doctors told me they thought he was a girl and I went shopping for frills and lace. You knew even then your plan and purpose for his life. You even sent your Son for mine. Please God, let him be safe."

Somehow I'm dressed and my husband pushes a rain jacket at me as we go down the stairs. I can't focus on the here and now. I see instead a curly-headed toddler in fuzzy red pajamas taking his first steps. I remember how he skipped the whole walking thing and went straight to running as though life was passing too quickly.

"God, is that what I do? Do I get caught on the fast spin of life and let it steal what's most important? I don't mean to. You've been so good to me. You've given me promises to depend on and grace to see me through. I need some of that grace now. God, where are you? Where's Torrey? Is he hurt? Is he still alive?

"Did I teach the most important things to my boys or was I too concerned about soccer practice, football games, swim lessons, and good grades? Do those things matter now? Did he call your name when he crashed?"

"Wait here while I get a flashlight," my husband says. He heads toward me, the light of the flashlight shining brightly as he checks the batteries.

Of course, he thinks of the batteries. I'm in a panic and he's checking the batteries. "We need to hurry, we may not have much time," I say. *Torrey was supposed to be at school. Maybe he loaned his truck to someone.* "I think it's raining harder," I turn to open the door.

"Hold on. Let's pray together before we go," Dean says and takes my hand.

My mind races. *He is a gift straight from you, God.* This strong man, so different in personality from me. Logical, grounded, centered, a good dad. With different parenting styles we still agree on the most important one, that of making God our guide on the journey. Dean's one more example of how you take care of me, Lord. Don't stop now. Let Torrey be safe.

"Dear Heavenly Father," Dean begins only to be interrupted by the ringing telephone.

I snatch the receiver. "Hello."

"Mamma."

How many times have I heard his voice say that word but never has it sounded so wonderful. I close my eyes and miss several sentences. He's saying something, I try to focus.

"I crashed the truck but don't worry, I'm OK. Dad may be upset; I think the truck's totaled. Why are you awake? It's 3:30 in the morning."

Relief washes over me in huge warm waves. I smile at my husband as I hand him the phone.

Thank you, God, for your amazing grace—grace that's there in the middle of the night. You're with me when trucks crash and fears consume. Thank you that I never have to travel the road alone.

Dr. Linda Mitchell is a professor at Mississippi State University where she works in areas of creative programming, youth development, and technology. She is a national motivational and educational speaker. She serves as Vice-Chair on the Board of Directors for the United States Congressional Award. Linda is a CLASS graduate.

Daunting Expectations

Cheryl Dore

Desiring to be gracious, my sister agreed to watch my four-year-old son and his baby sister at our home so my husband and I could enjoy a night out together. It seemed a reasonable option, although my children had not interacted with their aunt a great deal in this capacity.

In returning home, she greeted us giving an account of her night with my son even before the door was shut. "I couldn't figure out what was wrong with Devin, why he wouldn't come out from the stairwell and join us," she said. She described him as being aloof and agitated. Evidently she had tried to reach him but failed. She went on to say, "He preferred not to interact with me, so I let him be."

I was apprehensive and somewhat guarded, but I pressed for more. Being an overly protective mom who did not leave her kids with sitters very often, I was eager to know exactly how the evening played out for him. I asked warily, "Did you ever get him to interact with you?"

"Well, that's the point," she said. "While getting him dressed for bed, I found a burn on his buttocks." Troubled by the fact he had been hurt while in her care she went on to say, "I think he distanced himself because he had been hurt and was trying to hide it." I imagine my countenance spoke a thousand words, as she then added hastily, "But he didn't say anything. I had no way of knowing he had been burned!"

My insides churned as I pictured the very large burn brazenly imprinted upon his tender flesh. I did a quick replay in my mind recalling scenes from numerous conversations I had with him. Recalling each time he had been warned, "Devin, you could fall back into the hot glass and get burned!" You can imagine the havoc playing on my emotions learning the thing I feared actually happened; how he would climb out of the steaming bath, drop the dampened bath towel and perch himself on the edge of the hearth in front of the hot glass door with a fire blazing.

My conversation with my sister continued with my rebuttal, "So, you're telling me he did not get a cold compress on the burn right away? He had no immediate relief?" It only seemed right to be emotionally charged, even if it meant interrogating my sister. I could only imagine his blistering skin, the gravity of the experience, and his fear to share his pain. His behavior was much like Adam and Eve, who hid from God in the garden, feeling vulnerable and exposed, having done the very thing God told them not to do.

In that moment and even for years to come I anguished over resurfacing thoughts of him being without my unconditional love when he needed it most. What greatly distressed me was my son had been hurt and I was not there to comfort him, or wipe his tears and tell him, "Everything will be okay." Compounded by his inability to share what he was going through. Not that he did the very thing he was told not to do. Did he hide fearing his actions deserved reprimand? Was he even old enough for such reasoning? Had my example fed his hesitation? It caused me to examine my parenting being predisposed to set unreasonable expectations for myself, with no tolerance for my own mistakes.

Just as I told Devin, "*If you do this, this could happen,*" God's Word tells us we will reap the fruit of our actions. One instance can be found in Psalm 66:18 (NIV), "*If I had cherished sin in my heart, the Lord would not have listened.*" This would be unfortunate, if it were not for another verse which says, "*If we confess our sins, he is faithful and just and will forgive us our sins and purify us from all unrighteousness*" (1 John 1:9). The *if's* from God's Word are quite extensive with each one assuring us there will be a reward or consequence. The ball is in our court as we make daily choices, often finding ourselves at the end of our ropes, wrestling inwardly, beating ourselves up when we do the very thing we know not to do.

What do we do with those thoughts and feelings? Do we remain hopeful, and trust in the unconditional love of God? Or do we hide as my son did, showing we are afraid to trust God with our fears and failures?

I learned at a very young age that mistakes were unforgivable. I can assure you there have been times when I identified wholeheartedly with my son's fear. The temptation is to feel deserving of our lot in life and settle into our circumstances agreeing they are warranted. It's not that we hide or hold onto failures fearing God's wrath, we just don't feel deserving of His goodness and grace when missing the mark—yet again!

Paul's message in Philippians was written to silence this type of interpersonal reasoning. He says,

> *Brothers, I do not consider myself yet to have taken hold of it. But one thing I do: Forgetting what is behind and straining toward what is ahead, I press on toward the goal (mark) to win the prize for which God has called me heavenward in Christ Jesus* (Philippians 3:13-15).

When we fall, or fail, God is not planning a punishment, but a rescue. He is a redeeming God. His greatest concern is not that we did the very thing He told us not to do. But that we are hurting. Being a Father whose love for us exceeds my love for my son, may we come out from hiding and approach the throne of grace boldly. He is waiting with open arms to comfort and console. To tell us, "Everything will be okay." May we not be distant, and aloof, and miss *the embrace of a Father who is near to those who have a broken heart* (see Psalm 34:18).

CHERYL DORE is an aspiring author, and a dynamic certified C.L.A.S.S. speaker. She is best known for being transparent and genuine. At the printing of this book she is serving Foursquare Women National updating Web content, offering resources equipping women in leadership in the local church. Cheryl can be contacted at cheryl_dore@msn.com

It's Time to Go

Dr. Rebecca Dowden

The Lord had said to Abram,
"Leave your country, your people
and your father's household
and go to the land I will show you" (Genesis 12:1 NIV).

I hugged my last therapy patient of the day goodbye, locked the door behind her, and fell to my knees. Tears poured down my face as I cried out to God for help. "Dear God, I'm exhausted. I don't know what to do. How can I go on?" Unfortunately, this was not the first time I had pleaded this prayer. Over the last six months, I had become desperate. I was sinking deeper and deeper into a hole of emotional and physical burn-out, begging God for direction, but my fears kept me from truly listening to his answer.

As a child, I never wanted to obey my mother when she told me it was time to leave the monkey bars and go home. I might have been forty-two years old, but I had the same problem: I couldn't leave.

That same night I got home, and I crumbled as I poured out my heart to my husband—again. "I'm dying. I can't do this anymore," I told him through my sobs.

"Honey, I hate to see you so miserable. What do you think God is wanting you to do?" my husband asked.

"I don't know." I was crying with frustration. "I'm so confused. I believe that God led me out of teaching and into counseling."

"But maybe He is leading you out of counseling now," he said.

"How can that be? *He* gave me these talents. *He* turned my life in a whole new direction in order for me to become a therapist, and on top of all that, my patients need *me*." Even as I said these last words, I knew they were not true. My patients needed God. However, I was gripped by so much fear I couldn't feel the truth or act on it. Like so many other nights during those months, I went to bed exhausted, confused, and afraid.

The next morning I sat in my car in front of my office, and a deep current of despair pulled me under. Through my tears, I dialed my husband's phone. "What am I going to do? I don't think I can physically do this again today."

"Sweetheart, please listen to what you're saying. You've expressed this heart-breaking pain to me so many times over the last few months, but I don't think you're listening to God. I know He will tell you what to do," my husband said. I knew he was right, of course, and I felt like I was listening with all my might but all I could hear were my own fearful thoughts taunting me. "Close your practice? No way! You'll be giving up. You'll let all your patients down. You'll be a failure. You're just not doing this right. Try harder. Buck up!"

In the weeks to come, my physical ailments began to speak louder than my emotional pain. My stomach hurt, my head ached, I couldn't eat, I couldn't sleep. I just couldn't take it any longer. One morning, with my tear-stained face in the pillow, I heard God speak to me as if He were whispering inside my ear, "My precious child, *My* grace is sufficient." I wasn't sure what

His grace would look like if I took the leap of faith and closed my practice, but I felt so broken I finally surrendered. I closed my practice and spent the next year lying on my own couch. I did nothing but let God restore my mind, body, and soul.

One year later, I opened an email from a former teaching colleague at my alma mater Houston Baptist University, where the teaching is student centered and Christian values are honored. "So," he wrote, "what are you up to these days?"

That was exactly the question I had been asking myself. "Not much." I wrote back and explained.

"Have you given any thought to going back to teaching?" he asked and told me that Houston Baptist was hiring new faculty.

A few weeks later, I walked into the department chair's office and knew I had come back home. Houston Baptist University offered me a professorial job in the English department four months later, and I saw the gift God had for me all along.

Like Abram, God called me to leave the place I knew, and go to a place He would show me. Even though I had been afraid to let go and follow Him, He never gave up on me. I'd like to say I will always trust Him. The truth is, a part of me may always be like that little girl who doesn't like to leave the park. But God showed me in a very real way how He is a loving Father who leads me home, even if He has to pry my fingers off the monkey bars. His grace *is* always sufficient.

REBECCA DOWDEN is an assistant professor of English at Houston Baptist University, a licensed professional counselor, and a writer. She is the co-founder of Abounding Love Ministries with her husband, Al Dowden. She loves helping others find healing and freedom in God's love. She lives with her family in Houston, Texas.

My God, My God, Why Have I Forsaken You?
Anita Agers-Brooks

Daddy often said, "You could wear a 500-dollar suit and look like a ragamuffin." It hurt my feelings, but as a small child my flare for mixing orange plaids and purple polka dots was soon forgotten as I went to play. My carefree spirit conflicted with Mom and Dad's strict parenting. I was independent from infancy. Even at six months old I insisted on feeding myself; food hitting my face more than my mouth.

Dad was a preacher during most of my childhood. People in the church watched me all the time as I tried to fit the mold of whomever I was around. I felt enormous pressure to make people happy.

When at church, many self-appointed grandmothers waited to catch me doing something wrong like running through the building or whispering during service. They didn't hesitate to scold me and often said, "You're the preacher's daughter, so behave yourself."

Other members gushed when at four years old I sang, "Sunlight, sunlight, in my heart today," before the church. As I grew, their syrupy fawning added self-inflicted pressure to be perfect. Every time I messed up, a weight of guilt followed.

At school and around non-Christian family members the atmosphere changed. They called me holier than thou and made fun of me because Dad was a preacher. I commonly heard, "Oh, I forgot you don't do that," or "Miss Goody Two Shoes is scared she'll go to hell." I felt unaccepted and ashamed when they taunted me.

Rebellion is a strange thing. I admired people who broke the rules. I thought they were courageous when they talked back to teachers or ran into class late. Still, deep down I also wanted to do the right thing. My mind battled daily between my conscience and a desire to fit in. It usually ended with me avoiding God altogether. I just couldn't seem to get a handle on obedience.

My struggle started when I was five years old riding the bus to kindergarten. I wore a red plaid dress with black shoes and white socks. Some older kids asked, "Why don't you wear pants like the other girls?"

"Because I don't like pants," the lie slipped off my tongue like oil through a funnel. They ribbed each other and chuckled, but the teasing stopped.

I took shallow breaths as I stared out the window, because I felt like a coward. We were poor and I was ashamed of that truth. All of my clothes were dresses handed down from people at church. They never sent pants.

As I got older, I began to play at the edge of the water in life's cesspool. I remember uttering a word that verged on profanity. When God didn't immediately strike me with lightning, I became braver. I enjoyed the approving laughter as I threw curse words into a sentence. Soon, I could cuss as well as the boys in school. I liked being someone who stood out in the crowd.

As a teenager I threw myself into every sport and extra-curricular activity our school offered. These events let me tell many "white" lies. I could always say practice ran late, or the game went over. The things I did under the cover of those lies would have saddened and disappointed my parents.

My God, My God, Why Have I Forsaken You?

It was odd how each wrong choice made it easier for me to cross other lines. I justified a few curse words with, "Everyone does it." Laughing at off-color jokes made me feel included. Drinking alcohol wasn't that bad. I told myself, *I just want to have a little fun.* Over-the-top flirting didn't hurt anyone, did it? Finally, I made some unspeakable decisions. I let man's impression supersede God's discretion.

I sought immediate gratification. Later, there were consequences when I confessed to my mom I might be pregnant at sixteen. Terrified, I thought she would tell me to get out. Instead she cried with me and said, "I am so sorry, I never wanted this to happen to you." I broke down in a mixture of relief and sadness.

God saw everything I did in secret. In His justice I experienced life-altering changes. They brought tears, pain, embarrassment, and grief. For me, and those I love, the price was high. We suffered judgment from others and financial trouble, as I was challenged to forgive myself.

Yet these very trials taught me more about God's grace than anything else. Apparently I have to learn things the hard way. Thankfully, *"The Lord disciplines those He loves and He punishes everyone He accepts as a son"* (Hebrews 12:6 NIV). Every time I was caught in my sin He brought it out in the open. Every time He convicted me to confess, He made me clean. I didn't have to worry about acceptance; His forgiveness guaranteed it.

As an adult I remember the lessons I learned the hard way and pray for mercy. I turned my back on Him and ran to a world that didn't really care about me. My "friends" deserted me when I needed help. I realize now that as I stumbled and fell, He was the one who picked me up and brushed me off. I think back to all the secret moments in my life that He watched. His Word is true when He explains in Luke 7:36-50, *He who is forgiven much loves much.*

Today I am able to say, "Lord, I love You with all of my heart. Thank You for the gift of faith and giving me grace instead of what I really deserved. I am grateful that though I ignored You in the past, You never abandoned me."

I don't know why God never gave up on me. If I had gotten what I deserved He would have said, "This one is hopeless, I don't want her anymore." But grace isn't about punishment; it is about surprising mercy at the hands of unimaginable love.

Sometimes that scared little girl still surfaces in my life. When she does, I run straight into the arms of God. He tenderly washes the dirt off, wipes the tears from my eyes, pulls the wisps of hair from my face, kisses my forehead, and holds me on His lap. He graciously says, "Daddy's here and Daddy loves you."

ANITA AGERS-BROOKS is a Communications Specialist, Certified Personality Trainer, Certified Team Training Facilitator, Productivity Specialist, public speaker, and writer. She lives in Missouri with her husband Ricky, and is the mother of two grown sons, and three delightful grandchildren. Her website is www.freshstartfreshfaith.org Contact her via email: abrooks@misn.com

How God Orchestrated My Life

Ruth Holland

I first heard God speak to me at the age of five. My mother had a series of children's Bible books. I was sitting on the floor going through the books, looking at the pictures. I suddenly heard a male voice. It was loud and deep, yet gentle. It said, "You are special."

I was not frightened but quickly turned around and saw no one. I didn't know who said it, but for the first time in my life, I believed that I was special. I knew I would do something special with my life. What I didn't know was how I could be special when every other voice in my life told me that I was nothing.

I don't blame my parents. They loved me in the only way they knew how. My mother was never home, because she was a workaholic. In her mind, your value came from all of the things you accomplished. I could only be special to her if I could be the best. I tried to understand, but instead I withdrew from my family.

With nine children in our family opportunities weren't exactly knocking on our door. No matter how much my mother worked it was never enough. We were poor and I was staring into the face of failure.

A year after my older sister's birth, my mother had a nervous breakdown after discovering that my dad had been having an affair with my aunt. They had five children at that time. Each of them were sent to live with different family members until my mother recovered.

After her discharge from the hospital she and my father reconciled. My mother went to nursing school. By the time I was born she was working the night shift and sleeping during the day. She justified this by saying it was the only way she could provide for us. I didn't feel justified, I felt neglected to the point of abandonment.

My father was an alcoholic. When my dad was home he was drunk more times than not. He was both physically and emotionally abusive to my mother and all of us children. Late one night he came home drunk. He pulled us out of bed and took me and my younger sister and brother to church in our pajamas. I was embarrassed, ashamed, and angry. We never went to church any other time, but that night as we stood in the cold outside a locked building I swore I would make something out of my life.

In high school the abuse at home led to depression and apathy. Education did not matter to me. School was not for learning, it was a place to be safe, away from my family. My sister and I would stay at school as late as we could trying to avoid home.

During Nursing School, I fell into one bad relationship after another. Eventually I met Paul. He loved me and I longed to please him. If he said I gained weight, I stopped eating. After we married he allowed me to work only part time. He wanted to make sure I could not make more money than he did. Paul was an alcoholic who smoked at least two packs of cigarettes a day. We had two children and by the time they were in school, they had developed respiratory problems related to second-hand smoke. Paul refused to keep the smoke out of our home. My children were getting sicker and I was sick of my life.

I had a good friend who was a Christian. I didn't understand how she could have so much joy even when things weren't always perfect in her life. One day I asked her about it and she told me about Jesus. She knew my life and suggested that I speak to her pastor. That afternoon she and her pastor prayed with me and I accepted Jesus Christ as my personal Savior. It was a beautiful experience. I literally felt butterflies in my chest. I was amazed when I could read the Bible with understanding. I was a Christian!

I prayed that God would convert Paul. I was hoping for something like Saul's experience on the road to Damascus. Something was changing in him. Unfortunately it was not for the better. Paul acted as if he was being tormented. He was angry and irrational. Eventually he confessed that he was having an affair.

I cried. I yelled. I threw him out. As he was leaving I fell to my knees. Sobbing, I asked God to show me why this was happening to me. I wasn't a bad person, I prayed, I went to church, I gave donations. God asked, "Now who is your God?"

I immediately realized I had made Paul the god in my life. I repented, begging God to forgive me for my idolatry.

Paul and I divorced. As a single mother, I had to work at the hospital as much as I could to support my children. Paul refused to pay child support. I learned to lean on the Lord for my every need. But I was getting lonely. I missed the companionship I had in my marriage. "O God," I prayed, "please take this loneliness from me or bring me a husband who will love me."

I knew I had to wait on God for the right husband. In the meantime I needed to know that God was there. I needed His presence in my life. I longed to feel and touch Him. I totally surrendered to His will.

Two months later I met Chuck. He had never been married, he had no children, and he had his own business. He was romantic and charming. I loved him immediately. My children adored him. Chuck fell in love with my children and cared as much for them as he did for me. He was the answer to my prayers—my gift from God.

During the darkest times in my life God had His hand on me, guiding and protecting me even before I knew Him. Chuck and I married on August 28, 2001. Today we serve the Lord together and our household is a household of faith.

RUTH HOLLAND is an RN from Whittier, California. She attends Regency Christian International Church. She received her Bachelor's in Theology from Vision International in 2006. Ruth enjoys spending time with her husband, Chuck, and her children, Jason and Rochelle. She values their love and support and hopes they know how much she loves them.

Sustaining Strength

Dr. Michelle L. Bengtson

I was looking forward to that "perfect" stage in life. After several years of a commuter marriage while I completed my medical training, I set my sights on life together again. Then I received the call that no daughter wants to get, much less from the woman she considers to be her best friend. My mother relayed through tears and gasps that doctors had diagnosed her with lung cancer.

She had surgery, time passed, and our hopes for her recovery improved. Soon thereafter, my first child was born and life was good. We became absorbed in all his "firsts"—his first smile, his first giggle, his first "mama" and "dada."

Then, during a routine physical, my husband's doctor ordered additional tests: blood work, CT scan, and ultimately a biopsy, which started two years of gut-wrenching heartache. "Your cancer is extremely rare," his doctor said. I'm not sure of everything he said next, but I remember clearly when he told us, "I am sorry, but I suggest you get your affairs in order, you have less than two years to live."

All I could see was that day when, as a little girl, I stood at my father's casket so that others could pay their condolences.

This time I would be the mother standing with her young fatherless child.

My husband's hand in mine brought me back to the present and immediately my driven personality started running down a list of things to do and people to call. I was a doer ... I had to do something. The hardest part of planning for the future was not knowing exactly what it would look like, or what I could do to change it.

We consulted several cancer specialists. The prognosis never improved, although we did pursue treatment options. We endured a twenty-hour surgery, months of convalescence, and chemotherapy for my husband. Tears streamed down my face at unforeseen times. I lost more weight than was safe for my petite frame. I lost count how many times I heard "I don't know how you do it." But I could cope much better if I just kept doing, achieving, accomplishing something. Yet there were times I couldn't even make a simple decision, my mind too sluggish to think about what to do next. I realize now, those were the times God graced me with renewing peaceful sleep, moments of unscheduled quiet, and laughter of a toddler oblivious to adult stress.

During Scott's convalescence we found out to our delight that I was pregnant. It might seem strange by any one else's opinion, but I was glad. Our first born was our spot of sunshine who, a moment or two at a time, allowed us to forget about the tornado that put our life in a whirl. In the uncertainty of Scott's future, the possibility of yet another ray of brightness helped us cope. The joy of baby giggles and grins helped me to look past the dark days that surrounded us when Scott was so ill he could barely lift his head off the pillow, days when he wanted to be left alone. When Scott was first diagnosed with his cancer, we determined in our minds that "next year" would be a better year, and this new life inside of me seemed to be confirmation of that.

Around Thanksgiving my mother's health abruptly worsened and doctors told us to come immediately. My brother and I stood vigil at the hospital. Days later, the severity of concern was gone. That was incomprehensible to her doctors, but not to us. In her weakened state, she whispered intently to her doctor's ear, "Jesus is the Great Physician!"

God truly blessed us when we gathered with the entire family for our first Christmas all together in our married lives, rejoicing in her recovery. We later realized how special that blessing was. Our first Christmas with the entire family would also be the last.

My heart felt deceived when we went for my routine pregnancy check-up. My doctor studied the sonogram screen.

"I'm sorry, Hon," my doctor said. "I can't find a heartbeat."

Later I sobbed into the phone, "Mom, please pray." I could barely get the words out to tell her why, but I was clinging to hope that the next day's higher level ultrasound would detect life. There was no heartbeat the next morning, and for a brief moment, I wished I had none either. Then I remembered myself as a little girl with no father, and I thought of my son. Now more than ever, he would need his mother.

During these months, my family and I supported each other through the torment of doctor's appointments, chemotherapy, bad hair days, and even no hair days. Even when times were bleak, my mother's eyes lit up whenever she saw my son, and his for her. He had learned to say the sweetest word to her ear, "Nana." I stayed busy caring for my toddler and my husband, working full-time, and trying to clear out our house of aerosols, potpourri, and any other offender of her frail lungs.

About two weeks later, I listened to my voicemail at work.

"Michelle, she's gone."

I dropped to the floor. I had just seen her. We had plans. We were going to shop together. Have afternoon tea. Bake Christmas cookies. My best friend was gone and so were many of my dreams, of which she was the star.

Friends and family offered condolences. I don't know if they knew how I felt. I continued to hear "I don't know how you do it." Some offered the advice to "just take it one day at a time." But I recall praying, "God, please help me to make it through the next five minutes." I didn't know how to catch my next breath. I didn't know what to say when people asked me how I managed. I didn't know how to fix it.

I didn't know.

I was a doer.

Zechariah 4:6 (NIV) says, "*Not by might nor by power, but by my Spirit, says the Lord Almighty.*" As long as I continued to try to be independent, do things in my own strength, I came up short, tired, and weak. It was only as I began trusting in Him to sustain me day by day, and moment by moment, that I began to understand.

It was in the days and weeks and months ahead I held on dearly to the Lord. That was all I knew to do. All I could do. But that was a new, fresh, and more comfortable doing. In my weakest moments, those when I didn't know what to do, I learned to rely on the strength of the Lord.

DR. MICHELLE BENGTSON is a neuropsychologist in private practice in Southlake, Texas. Through professional and personal experience she has learned to see the joys of life through traumatic situations. Michelle has been married for twenty years to her husband, Scott, and is the mother to two wonderful boys. www.texnant.com; drbengtson@verizon.net

Write down the revelation and make it plain on tablets so that a herald may run with it.

Habakkuk 2:2

The Pony-Tailed Guy Goes to School
Lawrence J. Clarke

I stepped out of the courthouse into a bleak, drizzly autumn day, tailor-made for a depressing movie scene.

A few minutes earlier, I was standing before a judge.

"Do you agree to the terms of this decree and to the dissolution of this marriage?"

I turned to my wife, whom we'll call "M." She stood a few feet away, partially obscured by her attorney. I finally caught her eye, but she just looked away.

"Yes," I mumbled. And that was that.

We had two children. Stephanie, my "Sweetie-Pie," was four, and Andrew, my "Buddy Boy," not quite two. Wednesday nights and every other weekend they visited my cheap one-bedroom apartment behind a supermarket in College Station, Texas, where I was a graduate student at Texas A&M.

I stopped attending our church not long after M and I separated. I tried a couple of other churches, but never got involved. I graduated from a small Christian college and served twice as a missionary before Stephanie was born, but I felt guilty for succumbing to the Big D, something I promised God I would never do. I was angry at M for divorcing me, and at myself for not fighting harder to save our marriage. I felt inadequate and helpless. I badly needed Christian fellowship, but shame and guilt kept me from the good people God could have used to help me.

I was on track for a university professorship upon graduation, but I couldn't afford to stay in school full-time, so I took a community college instructor position. I worked half-heartedly on my dissertation and played songwriter gigs at night. At first I felt uncomfortable in some of the venues, but convinced myself God was using me to minister to the regulars.

One night, performing in a smoky bar, I sang these lyrics that I penned. "I could see my mama in her room down on her knees, praying to sweet Jesus to keep watching over me." One woman, who was fairly rowdy most of the night, quieted down and listened closely. When I finished, she walked up and gave me a hug.

"God put you here to speak to my heart," she whispered through her tears.

I wish all my songs were as effective, but I usually catered to the typical bar crowd. I soon came to prefer the nightclub scene to the churched community. These people seemed less pretentious, and somehow more real.

Five years later, I foolishly married someone six weeks after our first date. Unfortunately, almost nothing she told me about herself was true. Within three months, her deceptions started to unravel, and I filed for divorce. We were married just long enough to produce a baby girl, Lauren, but the Big D had struck again. I was now a two-time loser paying child support to two different women. I seriously considered calling Jerry Springer and volunteering to be a guest.

Between my personal struggles I somehow finished my dissertation and found a tenure-track professor position in New Mexico, half-way between San Francisco, where M moved the previous year, and Houston, where Lauren's mom lived. After a year, though, I reluctantly submitted my resignation.

"I'm so sorry," I told the dean, tears streaming down my face. "I love my job, but I need to be closer to my daughter."

I spent a decade in graduate school to earn that position, but I could think of no other option. Lauren's mom was unstable—financially and otherwise—and my little girl needed her daddy. I landed a technical writing job in Austin and saw Lauren every other weekend. Over the next four years, I performed regularly and released two CDs. I succeeded enough to quit my job and teach part-time, and grew my hair into a ponytail, which together with a black cowboy hat became my trademark image.

Unfortunately, I also fell into another disastrously dysfunctional relationship. Stephanie and Andrew did not approve of my lifestyle or my girlfriend, and eventually refused to visit me.

Then one Sunday I awoke with a strong urge to go to church. There was a tiny country church down the road from my house, so I dragged myself out of bed and slid into the back, hoping to remain unnoticed. I tried to look busy, so I lowered my head to read the bulletin and saw the following verse printed on the cover:

"Have I not commanded you? Be strong and courageous. Do not be terrified; do not be discouraged, for the Lord your God will be with you wherever you go" (Joshua 1:9, NIV).

I blinked twice. Twenty years earlier I wrote a song based on that verse! I thought I was writing it for other people, but now the lyrics spoke to *me* as I slowly remembered them:

Has he not commanded you? Be strong and courageous.
Has he not commanded you? Do not be afraid.
For the Lord your God is with you wherever you go,
helping you to grow and showing you His way.
Yes, the Lord your God will never let you go,
no matter how you've failed him or how far you've run away ...
Just keep His Word hidden safe within your heart,

Never turning to the left, never turning to the right.
and you will know the joy of living in His love,
a joy to keep you going even through your darkest night.

Failed Him. Run away. I realized it was time to stop running. Tears filled my eyes as I felt the Holy Spirit's loving embrace. I can't remember his exact words, but Pastor Jim's gentle and encouraging preaching style helped comfort my wounded heart. I started attending every Sunday, earning the nickname "The Pony-Tailed Guy" from some of the members. After a few weeks the worship leader invited me to play guitar with the praise team. I reluctantly agreed, humbled that God could have any use for someone like me.

A joy to keep you going even through your darkest night. Little did I know, but my darkest night was yet to come. I became convicted that the relationship I was in needed to end, and finally mustered up the courage to break it off. Not long after, I met a talented songwriter who also played flute. Cindy and I immediately clicked. I invited her to perform with me on a live radio interview, and we began spending most of our free time together.

A few weeks later, she mentioned that we had been seeing each other exactly one month.

"That's all? It seems like I've known you much longer."

"Me too," she said, "I feel as giddy as a school girl." Things were definitely going well, and it seemed God was rewarding me for my recent obedience.

A few days later, I stopped by for lunch, then stayed at Cindy's apartment working on a new song while she ran some errands and picked up her son from school.

Four hours later, she still wasn't home. The phone rang, but the machine picked up before I could reach the receiver. It wasn't her.

"We're calling to express our condolences, as we heard that Cindy passed away this afternoon. If there's anything we can do, call us at …"

I reached for the phone, but too late. I stood motionless for a few minutes, trying to comprehend what I just heard, then walked outside, the words still ringing in my head.

Just then Cindy's son walked up the sidewalk. I breathed a sigh of relief.

"Hey Ethan, how are ya?" I asked.

Silence.

"Uh, where's your mom?"

"Oh, Lawrence, come inside. I need to tell you something."

That precious twelve-year-old boy sat me down on the couch and pulled up a chair.

"My mom is dead."

"Wha—How?!?"

"We pulled out of a driveway and a truck hit her side of the car. She died before the ambulance got there."

I cried for days, asking God why He would let this happen. I felt like I knew Cindy so well after so many hours of sharing our lives and hopes and dreams, even though we only dated for barely over a month.

Although I just finished a new album, I didn't have the heart to promote it. I cancelled all my upcoming shows and flew to New England to visit family. I tried to remember the happiness Cindy and I shared so briefly, but it was all just a blur. I didn't have the slightest idea how to explain to anyone what I had just experienced, so I didn't.

Even though I was still grieving terribly, Pastor Jim's sermons sunk in. The lyrics from the Joshua 1:9 song also provided some comfort and guidance:

Has he not commanded you? Be strong and courageous. This was not a request; it was a command. And even though those words were written thousands of years earlier, they spoke to me now in my "darkest night."

"What was I to do now?" I thought.

Do not be afraid. But I *was* afraid. I had once again placed my hopes in another person rather than in God. "You're just a walking failure waiting to happen," the voice in my head kept saying. But more lyrics came back to me:

For the Lord your God is with you wherever you go, helping you to grow and showing you His way. Yes, He *was* with me. He never left me. *I* left Him. But like the wise Father that He is, He knew I would, and He used these events to prepare me for the next phase of my life, which would be lived not my way, but His.

That phase took shape over the next year, and included a return to writing and teaching as a professor at a Christian university, as well as a more active role in Lauren's life, since the school was in Houston!

I now teach subjects I love, to students who (mostly) care, at a university dedicated to providing a Christian liberal arts education. I host a café series that features songwriters, poets, and authors. I read my creative works and perform my songs in schools, libraries, churches, and community centers across the country.

Stephanie and Andrew are now in college, and my relationship with both of them has greatly improved. Lauren, my little "Brown-Eyed Girl," is in the sixth grade and brings great joy to my life. And if those blessings weren't enough, God has also provided me with a wonderful Christian wife, Kristen, whose godly character and encouraging spirit are a wonderful gift to me and my children.

The joy of living in His love. After trying for years on my own, I finally understand what true joy really is. I know my circumstances can change at any moment, but I am now equipped with the confidence that I can turn to Him, rather than the ways of this world, to find fulfillment or comfort.

Recently I heard someone say we experience God's mercy when we don't get what we deserve, and His grace when we get what we don't deserve.

"Yeah," I said, nodding my head in agreement. "Yeah."

The Pony-Tailed Guy Goes to School

Lawrence J. Clark is the proud father of three kids and four cats, and husband of an amazing wife. He teaches writing and literature at Houston Baptist University, and spends summers and vacations at the family retreat in New Mexico. He can be found online at www.lawrencejclark.com, www.singingpoetguy.com, and www.hiswitness.org.

My Parting of the Red Sea

Ruby Heaton

I stopped my car in the middle of the street. I felt as if I was in a dream. I looked around and noticed blood all over the window, dashboard, and steering wheel. It was my blood. I was leaning into the horn in between yelling and pushing Marcos out of my car. He was telling me to stop before the police came. I told him that is exactly what I wanted to happen. He got out and ran down the street.

I drove off to a friend's house drenched in my own blood, wondering how I ever got to this point. I am a happy, loving, kind, good, and moral person. How did I end up in this nightmare with no escape?

I had pushed all the memories far back in my mind, until the question was asked in Bible study class, "Did your ever have a parting of the Red Sea?" Then the memories found their way back out of the dark corners where I had hidden them. It was a frightful time in my life, one I would choose to forget. Yet I felt I needed to expose this story to shed light for the benefit of others.

I met Marcos when my girlfriend, Tanya, and I were on our way to college. He was driving beside us in an ambulance. He was a paramedic with a great smile. We managed to connect, and I found out he lived a block away from me. He told me he had been watching me for a while because he liked me. Funny I had never noticed him before.

Marcos was tall, handsome, and built. He had a way with words. Everyone said he had a lot of charisma. He would smile, and women would melt and do anything for him. He did not have that effect on me, and I guess that is why he was so interested in me. He did all sorts of sweet things for me. He would play the guitar and sing to me, in person and on the phone. I guess he sang his way into my heart, because before long I fell for him.

One day my girlfriend, Tanya, and I were going to breakfast, and Marcos showed up and wanted to tag along. I was surprised at how he had suddenly appeared, but he handled it so smoothly. Marcos showed up at my work and school; he was always watching me. It got to a point where I could not look at or talk to another male. He would blow up if any male talked to me, even a cashier at the market. I was suffocating. He was no longer just scaring me, he was getting physical.

I tried breaking up with Marcos several times, but it never went well. He would get angry and start to threaten me. One time when I had managed to break up with him, my father, and my uncle let him in the house, because I would not let him in. Both my father and uncle told me to be nice to him, and they insisted I go out with him. They practically threw me out the door. He made them feel sorry for him.

Another time when I tried to tell my father what he was doing to me, Marcos pulled me into a corner of our dining room. He hit me, with the house filled with guests, and no one even noticed. He told me, "You see how easy it is? Be quiet or it will get worse."

One day in desperation, I went to one of the nuns at my school, and I told her a little about what he had been doing to me. She said "Oh, no, not that nice young man. I do not believe it."

My Parting of the Red Sea

She left me with my mouth hanging open. He had so much charisma I could not even get a nun to help me. Marcos broke into our family home while we were on a family vacation, and destroyed all of my clothes because I went with my family. He slept on my porch in the rain to spy on me. He beat me until I did not even recognize myself in the mirror. I cried, thinking, *What if my face stays like this?*

We called the police several times, and they told us they could do nothing. This took place before the laws changed; there was no help for the abused. I was shocked, hurt, upset, and scared. I had no option but to stay in my situation.

Marcos and I went to a family party, and he said, "Ruby, let's go for a walk. I need some air." As soon as we walked out and were in front of the neighbors white picket fence, he stopped walking, turned to look at me, and his whole demeanor changed. His eyes bulged, his face got red, and he started to yell. I had no idea why he was angry. He reached for my neck, and he grabbed the gold chain with the cross my parents had bought me. Then, he tore it off my neck, spun around, and tossed it as far as he could.

I was in shock because my cross did not protect me. I always wore a cross, thinking it had power to protect me. As fear and confusion spun in my head, I heard a voice saying, "Ruby, a cross cannot protect you. There is no power in it. But I am with you."

At one point, my father said, "Ruby, get rid of him or go live with him." Knowing I could not get Marcos to leave me alone, I packed a few things and showed up on Marcos's doorstep. I told Marcos, "Okay, you want me, here I am. I was upset with my parents for pushing me out, and they were tired of Marcos. And so was I.

Abusive people usually have two sides to them. I knew Marcos loved me; he could be very sweet and protective. We would laugh, joke around, and have fun together. But it was as if he was two different people. He could go from one extreme to the other. His relationship with his mother should have been a sign to me. Now I know that the way a man interacts with his mother is a good reflection of how he will treat his partner. I learned many things the hard way. I had jumped into the relationship too soon.

We rented a cute little house, got married, and decided we should attend a Christian church. We joined a prayer group with some church leaders. They were kind, loving, and giving. I was touched and impressed with their ways. We went on a church sponsored marriage retreat, and things got better for a while. I had been raised Catholic, so this learning to walk with Christ was something new. It was exciting. I learned I could actually talk to God.

Due to a work related injury, Marcos went on workers compensation. The company hired investigators to follow him. He started doing strange things, like sleeping in closets. He said, "I have to hide. Everyone is following me." He would not leave the house in the day. He threatened me with a big kitchen knife and accused me of following him.

As I held our newborn son, Marcos threw something at me, almost hitting our baby. I remembered what God had dropped into my spirit that time with the cross, and I started to cry out to God to save us. I talked Marcos into letting me take the baby for a visit with my parents. Once I was at my parent's house, I told my father some of the things he was doing to us. My father said, "Stay here. You can't go back there."

I asked, "Are you sure, Dad? You know how Marcos can get?"

My dad said, "I'll get out my shotgun. You and the baby cannot go back. " Marcos called a couple of hours later. He threatened me and told me to get back home.

I said, "No!" And I hung up.

I cried out, "God if you're real, protect us and make a way out." God answered my cry. He became real to me that day as he parted my Red Sea and delivered me to a safe land. After all those years and all the tears, the nightmare ended. Marcos left and I was free!

My sister asked me one day," How did you do it, Ruby? You were alone with a newborn, yet you were so happy.

I told her," I found God. He was with me then as he is now. I have never been alone since I found God."

In Deuteronomy 4:29, God tells us how to seek Him. We are to seek Him with all our heart and soul. When we get honest and desperate, He allows us to find Him. This was the first time I had seen God's hand move in such a powerful way.

When Marcos was gone, my sister took me back to my get some of my things out of our house. We grabbed all we could. That was the last time I went through those doors. God shut the doors to that part of my life, and He opened new doors. God has done so much for me. God has opened ministry doors for me to speak, teach, and reach out with his love to hurting people. He even opened doors so I could minister to women in shelters. I know their pain and confusion, and I show them the way home.

RUBY HEATON is a partner in Destiny Defenders Ministry—teaching, coaching, prayer, and healing. A Class Communicator, she has a Associate Degree of Biblical Studies and writes non-fiction and poetry. She is a mother of four. Contact her at rubtues2000@yahoo.com. Visit her blog: awriterforgod.blogspot.com.

God's Waiting Room

Ginger O'Neill

Have you ever felt like no one was listening? Have you ever felt like God wasn't listening when you prayed? Welcome to God's waiting room!

I have felt the pain of being in God's waiting room. For fifteen years, I prayed for my unsaved husband. During those years I struggled with the waiting. I didn't understand why God didn't just zap him with a mighty dose of his Holy Spirit. It made no sense to me why it was God's will to wait. In 2 Peter 3 (NASV), I read, "The Lord is not slow about his promise, as some count slowness, but is patient toward you, not wishing for any to perish but for all to come to repentance." As I read that I didn't understand why God was waiting and not answering my prayer. The most logical explanation I could figure out was it must be my fault.

As the wife of an unsaved husband I often found myself in a state of confusion. Many thoughts robbed my joy of a personal relationship with Jesus. I found myself thinking how much easier it had been before I gave my life to Christ. At least then John and I had enjoyed the same things. The only thing we enjoyed together now was our daughter, Christina. I could not help wondering what kind of example he was for her.

There were times I thought of running away but I knew I didn't want to run away from my life with John. I just wanted him to be a part of the most special part of my life, my relationship with Jesus.

Even though God had blessed me with so many wonderful friends there was a loneliness that at times I thought I couldn't bare. I was in God's waiting room and I didn't know how much longer I could take it. I was lonely, confused, and disappointed because I had prayed and God hadn't answered my prayers.

In 1993 my youngest sister, Crystal, died of cancer. It gave me great comfort to know that she was in heaven and I would see her again. My comfort soon became fear: I didn't have assurance of John's eternity. I began to pray even more fervently for my husband to believe in the Lord.

As I pleaded with him to go to church it seemed that he became even more resistant. My pleading soon became nagging. Nagging didn't work.

I looked at the situation and thought, "This is one stubborn man and the only way he is going to change is if I get involved and help God." I believed the Scripture that says, *"Faith comes by hearing and hearing by the Word of God"* (Romans 10:17). Since John wasn't reading the Bible or going to church I thought I'd better take things into my own hands. I wrote Bible verses on index cards and placed them throughout the house. My imagination went wild as I excitedly posted memory verse cards on the refrigerator, lights switches, mirrors, and even toilet lids. Every time I went to a Christian retreat I purchased books and strategically placed them near his nightstand or easy chair. I also bought cassette tapes of Christian messages and put them in the car ready to play when he turned the car on. My husband thought I was some kind of nut. He just tossed them in the backseat, some of them were never found.

Many people tell me how wonderful I am because I prayed for my husband for fifteen years. However, in reality, it took fifteen years for God to change me first. I was so caught up in what I needed and what I wanted that I was not trusting God.

One night I was sitting in church and tears began to flow. I wasn't really sure why I was crying so I began to think about all the reasons I had for the tears. One by one I brought all of my reasons before the Lord and asked; "Lord, is this why I am crying?"

Each time the Lord said, "No."

With tears running down my face I left the sanctuary to regain my composure.

I was drawn back to that holy place. God and I had some unfinished business. I quietly slipped in, sat on the back pew and prayed, "Lord, I'm not leaving here until You tell me why I am crying." I sat there waiting with greater anticipation than I had ever experienced. His presence was so real, I was sure He was going to give me an answer. I waited, afraid to move. I didn't want to miss what He had to say.

Then in a still, small, yet undeniable voice the Lord began to speak to my spirit, "Ginger, the reason you are crying is because you always have to have control." I was stunned. This was not at all what I had expected to hear from the Lord. I had always considered myself a compliant person, a people pleaser, and considerate of all authority, especially the Lord. I could not imagine what He meant when He said I always had to have the control. I thought I was yielded, yet the Lord was telling me that I was in His way.

After a few seconds of shock and embarrassment, I called out to God again and asked, "Well, Lord, what do you want me to do?"

In a very clear and direct way He said, "There you go again, Ginger. It's not what I want you to do. Just be still and know that I am God." God got my attention that night. Although it was hard to have the Lord rebuke me so strongly, I knew it was true and I had to let go of the control and surrender everything to the Lord. I had to believe that He holds my marriage and my husband in His hands. I had to release my grip.

That night my faith to trust the Lord was raised and I had greater faith and trust in the Lord to do the right thing at the right time.

Soon after that, a group of dear friends surprised me with a house-warming party. I was humbled when Maria said, "Ginger this party is in your honor" and even more humbled when each one of them prayed a prayer over my family and my home. For years I thought no one knew how much I was hurting. For years I thought if only someone would pray for John. But it seemed no one noticed.

The Lord was moving and I knew I could trust Him. I was not surprised when the Lord prompted me to ask John to go church.

I remember John's face so clearly when I asked him if he'd like to go to church. As he stood there in the kitchen, his jaw literally dropped with surprise because God had prepared his heart. Then he said, "Yes I would like to go but not tomorrow because I have golf plans." It was hard to believe that he really wanted to go.

I hesitated asking him again and didn't bring it up again all week until the following Saturday night. Once again I took a step of faith and asked him if he would like to go to a church near our new home. I couldn't believe it when he said yes. All night I prayed and held on to the little bit of faith and thought *will he really go to church?* The next morning I was half dressed and he was still sleeping so I told the Lord, "I'm not waking him up. If you want him to go you get him up." Amazingly, my husband got up and was ready.

As we walked into the church he grabbed my hand and began to sing out very loudly. I looked at him and could not believe what I was hearing. I was even more surprised when John wanted to meet the pastor.

The following week, I thought he wouldn't go back. But again the next Saturday night I asked, "Did you want to go to that church again?" Once again, he said that he wanted to go.

That Sunday, November 24, 1996, as our daughter Christina and I stood hugging each other and crying, we watched John walk down the aisle to give his life to Jesus. A man sitting behind us, tapped me on the shoulder and said, "He needs you to go down there." I had always dreamed of going to the altar with him but I found myself telling the man, "This is between John and God."

Twenty minutes later he came out of the prayer room with a new light in his eyes and a sweet grin on his face. He looked at me and said, "Now don't expect me to be perfect." I hugged him knowing it was not my husband's perfection but God's perfect plan unfolded before my eyes.

Today, John is a Promise Keeper, plays his trumpet in the church orchestra, and loves to tell others about Jesus. When I start to take control, the Lord quietly reminds me to be still and know that He is God.

When we are in God's Waiting Room it is easy to get discouraged and become weary. But God is faithful and your name may be called next.

GINGER O'NEILL is a teacher, conference speaker, and author who shares from her heart with warmth and transparency at retreats and conferences. www.gingeroneillministries.com. She is a graduate of the University of South Florida with a BS in Special Education and a Masters in Educational Leadership. Ginger and her husband, John, live in Seminole, Florida.

Souvenir

Pam Morrison

 The people of Nicaragua decorate simple wooden crosses with vivid scenes of village life. Centrally placed is a Hispanic-looking Christ figure with outstretched arms. Every open space around him is crammed with red-roofed, white adobe houses, clusters of farm animals, and men and women carrying baskets of produce. Like all folk art, these crosses delight the eye with the brilliance of their reds, blues, greens, yellows, and bold black outlining that enhances the idyllic quality of the images.
 I was on my first mission trip to Nicaragua with a para-church relief group, Rainbow Network. I wanted to bring one of these crosses home to decorate my office. It would be so striking hanging on a wall as a remembrance of the trip. The mission group's director assured me that we could find one. In fact, we could combine that errand with one of their missional tasks of the day.
 Our team was temporarily idle on our first morning, waiting for further work arrangements to be made. In light of this, I joined Dr. Glenda and a driver, both Nicaraguans, to go out and pick up a boy to bring him back to the mission office to receive a new wheelchair. Wheelchairs from the United States, even used

ones, are luxury items with their padding, brakes, and comfortable designs. The wheelchair set aside for this boy was like new, with a blue padded back and seat and broad silver foot pedals. It was easily available in countless U.S. hospitals.

I headed out to the jeep with Dr. Glenda and the driver with the information that we would stop first to look for a cross and then go to the boy's house. I felt a little uncertain as I headed off alone with my two new Nicaraguan friends, neither of whom spoke English, as I speak only a few words of Spanish. However, I was delighted to have a chance to get the cross I longed for. I sat in the back of the jeep and they chattered together in a friendly, fully Spanish conversation. Soon we stopped before a building which was clearly a workshop. The door stood open. Male voices drifted out accompanying the sound of saws and hammers buzzing and pounding.

This was no quaint gift store with charming Latino gift items under counters. This was a humble factory and clearly masculine territory. Tables, cabinets, wooden furniture, and other simple items were being made in this cramped space. The floor was bare but for piles of sawdust. Fresh cut wood filled the air with a pungent odor.

A silence fell as we entered. The men stopped working and stared. Dr. Glenda and our driver began to speak rapidly to them. There were no colorful souvenir crosses here, just plain bare wood, oak and pine. I shook my head and backed out. Dr. Glenda and the driver looked puzzled and shrugged. This frustrated American shopper and two Nicaraguans got back in the jeep, all of us quiet.

We drove out of the small, rural town into the countryside. What had been a rather poor road became no road at all. This would be a constant in our Nicaraguan experience. Roads were often dry washes, rutted, narrow, dusty. We were driving through these parched stream beds, farther and farther away from my sense of security, the rest of the American team. The simple effort of being unable to communicate about the cross left me unsettled.

For the first time, I felt like a foreigner.

The houses were no longer houses, but scavenged materials—cardboard, corrugated tin, bits of wood. Now I was seeing poverty such as I had never seen before and I felt uneasiness in this place with a different culture and different people and such raw need. We were driving deeper and deeper into this strange country of what Jesus would call "the least of these." Though a Christian given to caring for others, as a middle class American, I felt off balance. This was not care at a distance. This was up close.

When we finally stopped in one of these ditch-roads, we were at the base of a small, steep hill and above were several makeshift houses. Dr. Glenda and the driver began to climb the hill and hesitantly I followed them to the top.

Dr. Glenda leaned her head into the doorway of one of the ramshackle huts in this Nicaraguan neighborhood and sang out, "Melvin! Melvin!" I sensed this was not the first time she had played this game of greeting. After a moment, a string of Spanish words wrapped in tones of kindness, welcomed us into this home, and we stepped into the shadows of the front room.

A spindly pre-teen boy sat in a wheelchair at the center of the hut. Melvin's current wheelchair was a horrible, outdated contraption, all metal, no padding, narrow seat, uncomfortable, ancient. His father crouched on the dirt floor by his side. I could see immediately that this young boy struggled with the most basic of life's needs. Arm movements consisted of random spasms and twitches. His head bobbled on unreliable neck muscles. Melvin smiled sweetly, but only with partial awareness in his eyes. Carefully, his father spooned small bites of rice into his yawning mouth, yet as much rice flowed down his chin as remained inside of it. A cloth was ever present in his father's other hand and he wiped away the viscous trail of food left behind after each bite was taken. Melvin seemed unaware of much, but he clearly recognized Dr. Glenda. His eyes brightened at her entry, and affection radiated between them

My uneasiness began to fade as I watched this poor man care for his son. A couple of other very young, half-dressed children sat on the ground nearby scooping bites out of their own bowls of rice. Melvin's father was one of the most tender men I have ever seen. His words were soft and low and soothing as he fed his disabled son. No amount of drooling tested his patience. There was nothing but love pouring out from this humble man to his vulnerable boy.

We waited, unhurried, for the arduous feeding process to be done. When the meal was over, Melvin's father brought out some snowy white socks. I think I must have gasped. Where did socks so pure white come from in this dirt-floored hovel? How did they get them so clean? I watched the father gently pull a sock on each foot.

Oh, to have a heart like his, able to love in the midst of nothing. And how great the grace of God that I was able to be a witness. My discomfort and sense of foreignness dissipated in the presence of God's love. We should have taken off our shoes.

We were standing on holy ground.

Melvin's father lifted him out of the antiquated wheelchair and we all walked down the hill to the jeep. Dr. Glenda climbed into the back with me. Mr. Espinoza gently cradled his son in the front seat and we rode off to obtain what was a great treasure for them—for that is how they received it—the new, blue wheelchair.

Soon after, a picture of Melvin, smiling crookedly, in an American-made wheelchair, surrounded by cheering Americans, graced the cover of the Rainbow Network newsletter. There was much rejoicing that day in the mission office.

Perhaps I did not buy the painted Nicaraguan cross, but I treasure the "snapshot" of the cross that remains in my heart—that of Melvin's father serving his son. Beneath it is the caption,

"I have set you an example that you should do as I have done for you ... Now that you know these things, you will be blessed if you do them" (John 13:15, 17 NIV).

PAM MORRISON is a Methodist clergywoman who has served five churches. She is currently on leave and is enjoying other areas of ministry such as Prison Fellowship ministry to inmates, and writing. Her husband, David, is a grant-writing consultant and former research scientist. They have a married son and a daughter and reside near Lawrence, Kansas. E-mail: revpmorrison@aol.com

Mirror, Mirror

Daphne Delay

The voice was not audible. Standing in front of my bathroom mirror, I sensed a voice tell me to look closer in the mirror. I was not a mature Christian at the time, so I'm not sure how I knew it was God speaking to me, but I had no doubt.

Our eyes serve as windows to our soul, the real us. We look into mirrors at our reflection all the time, but we only see our exterior. Yet how we view ourselves will have the greatest impact on our life than any other thing. *"For as he thinks in his heart, so is he"* (Proverbs 23:7 NKJV). Everything runs off our inner image. However, when God looks at each of us He has the ability to look straight into our hearts because that is who we truly are. *"As in water face reflects face, so a man's heart reveals the man"* (Proverbs 27:19).

As I looked into the mirror at my reflection, God told me to look closer. I looked at my face, my hair, my body, and my clothes, expecting to find something wrong (again). I had always been self-conscience about my appearance and what others thought of me. But God said "No. Look close. Look deep into your eyes."

As I moved closer to the mirror and looked into my own eyes, I looked at another person. The eyes in the mirror reflected a girl who knew my innermost thoughts, fears, disappointments, hopes, and dreams. For years I tried to hide her because she was the guilty one who made all the mistakes. I hid her away while I focused on the exterior part of myself that others saw; the part that fit the world's pattern. I thought I could make the outside look good, regardless of how I felt inside.

As I stood there within an inch of the mirror, looking at nothing but those eyes—eyes reflecting great sorrow, God said, "Now tell her you love her and you forgive her."

I couldn't form the words. How many times had I silently cried out in my heart for God's deliverance? In my mind, a glass box had imprisoned me. Now standing face to face with the culprit, I was alarmed at who held me captive. I thought God held the key to my glass box. I thought the box was punishment for my failures. I could see God on the outside. I could see everyone else and I envied them. They must have all been perfect. "Be grateful," I would tell myself. "God has allowed you to come this far. Don't ask for more," and I never did. Yet now here I stood with the answer to my silent prayer. The key had always been in my hand.

Glued to the eyes looking back at me, I remembered horror stories I had heard about abused children locked in closets. The eyes in my mirror belonged to someone locked away, unloved and unforgiven. A steady stream of tears poured from my eyes for almost an hour as I tried to unlock the glass box.

In one sentence God showed me that although I had accepted His Son as my Savior and received His promise for eternal life in heaven, I had never accepted His forgiveness for my sins. I did not feel worthy of such forgiveness. Didn't He know all I had done? Didn't He know how many times I had failed? How could He forgive me? This kind of love and forgiveness was beyond my comprehension.

Alcohol, promiscuity, and drugs had tainted my young life. My home life had not been a bad one, just lacking in Christian morals and guidelines. Due to low self-esteem I struggled with telling people no. I lived in a vacuum of comparison, striving for the goal of perfection and approval. Becoming a Christian didn't lessen my insecurities. I found myself still trying to measure up, and I didn't like who I saw in my mirror every day. Not only had I failed at fitting into the world's pattern, but now I struggled with fitting into the image of a perfect *Christian*. Wrestling with guilt and shame over past sins, my condemnation compounded when I became pregnant outside of marriage shortly after becoming a Christian.

"Tell her you love her and you forgive her," God said. I held the key.

Contrary to what I thought in my heart, after much effort and many tears, I said those words: *I love you and I forgive you.*

In front of my mirror, God revealed His truth: *"If any man be in Christ Jesus, he is a new creation; the old has passed away, behold, all things have become new"* (2 Corinthians 5:17). At salvation my inward self had been drastically changed. The struggle I felt was between this inward person who had been forgiven and the old sinful one who had never been laid to rest.

As a child, my dad made my brother and I pull weeds. Some weeds could be pulled up easily because they had very little roots. Others took a lot of pull and effort because they had deep roots. Weeds with roots left in the ground will grow back. In His wisdom, the Lord knew my guilt and shame were deep-rooted. Saying the words, *I love you and I forgive you,* only scratched the surface. My problem had to be uprooted with sincerity. In other words, I had to mean what I said.

I don't know if another hour passed, but after more effort and tears, a second and heartfelt confession did the job. In that moment, the door of my glass box swung open. Like the unloved child released from the closet, the girl in my mirror was finally free from unforgiveness.

I had been unable to see how insecurities, feelings of low self-worth, fears, failures, disappointments, and attempts to be someone I thought everyone wanted me to be created the walls of my glass box. I built these walls out of a lack of knowledge of God's Word and His view of me. I did not understand my freedom in Christ.

"Tell her you love her and you forgive her." The voice was not audible, but His words forever changed my life. How we view ourselves will have a greater impact on our lives than any other thing.

Look in the mirror.

DAPHNE DELAY is the founder of Mirror Ministries. She is a Bible teacher, author, and respected speaker. Her passion is righteousness and our identity in Christ. This truth became her greatest revelation, and now her greatest joy comes from sharing this truth with others and seeing them understand it for themselves. www.mirrorministries.org

Living with the Giant

Cynthia Zahm Siegfried

I am living with a giant in my home ... and he is not jolly or green. He invaded my life six years ago the day my husband was diagnosed with lung cancer. When I recovered from the shock of his arrival and realized he intended to stay, I faced a dilemma. Should I get to know him better to prepare for his next attack? Should I make a battle plan to slay the nasty interloper? Should I try to ignore him and pray he might disappear as mysteriously as he arrived?

I chose the last option and finally became accustomed to his presence. But I never, ever forget he is here. I tiptoe around him because at any minute he might awaken, ravenous and threatening. *Will he devour me in one large bite or be satisfied with a little snack to hold him over while he returns to hibernation?* Sometimes he is so quiet; I think he might be dead. Then he stirs, rears his ugly head, and comes back even more ferocious than before.

I know that God must have left the door unlocked allowing the beast to enter. And I know God is able to protect me from the *"terror of the night"* and *"the pestilence that stalks in darkness"* (Psalm 91:5, 6 NIV). Unfortunately head-knowledge doesn't take the tension out of life with the giant. This brazen trespasser refuses to be ignored.

The giant's presence in our home creates constant stress. We agonize while waiting for test results. We struggle with life and death decisions. We haggle with insurance companies and worry about finances. Only the Word of God drowns out the giant's "fee, fie, foe, fumming." Only the grace of God gives us hope of slaying him.

God strengthens me in the battle with my Goliath just as He strengthened David. I don't spend nights weeping in my pillow or days biting my nails. From the day I heard the dreaded word "cancer," I have slept peacefully, relying on His promise in Proverbs 3:24, *"When you lie down you will not be afraid; when you lie down your sleep will be sweet."* Peaceful sleep is a miracle when the monster's snores echo throughout the house.

God has granted me the *"peace that passes understanding"* (Philippians 4:7) because *"I cast all my fears upon Him."* Yet while the giant hovers over me, I live with stress. Can I really experience peace and stress at the same time? Are fear and stress different?

Fear is almost always non-productive, immobilizing, and debilitating—a powerful rush of water from a broken dam. God tells us in Isaiah 41:10, *"Do not fear for I am with you."* He gives this command because fear robs us of the joy He provides. When the doctor told us that my husband had Stage IV lung cancer, I was so afraid I shook for months. I was barely able to get food past the lump in my throat. I believe my fear came from Satan, not God, because God doesn't give us a *"spirit of fear"* (2 Timothy 1:7).

Stress is like Chinese water torture with the victim scarcely aware of the first few drips but eventually worn down by the unremitting pressure. Since the giant moved in, I have felt this same kind of constant pressure. But stress, unlike fear, can be a positive force. God sometimes allows stress in our lives for our own good. Paul says in Romans 5:3-5, *"we know that suffering produces perseverance; perseverance, character; and character, hope."* Just as years of physical pressure changes coal into a precious gem, living with the giant is molding me into the person God wants me to be.

In college I learned about Hans Selye, the "Einstein of medicine." He was a famous physician who studied what happens to living things when they are stressed. First the organism experiences the "alarm reaction." I had a three-alarm reaction to the cancer diagnosis. The next stage, according to the theory, is resistance, a period in which the initial stress symptoms lessen. I was adjusting to life with the giant. Finally, comes the period of exhaustion, followed by death if the exhaustion continues. As a caregiver I have been exhausted countless times. We only grow when we are stretched. But there is a point of diminishing returns. Too much tension breaks the rubber band or stretches it beyond usefulness.

Selye may have been the Einstein of medicine but he didn't know how to recover from this state of exhaustion. Fortunately, Jesus does. *"Come to me all you who are weary and burdened and I will give you rest"* (Matthew 11:28).

God doesn't promise a stress-free life, but He does promise to provide strength and comfort in times of overwhelming pressure.

> *We have this treasure in jars of clay to show that this all-surpassing power is from God and not from us. We are hard pressed on every side, but not crushed; perplexed, but not in despair; persecuted, but not abandoned; struck down, but not destroyed"* (2 Corinthians 4:7-9).

People often comment on my strength in coping with the unremitting pressure of my husband's terminal illness. The strength is not mine. This jar of clay is designed to crack and break, but the grace of God holds it together.

Living with cancer, I lumber along in a state of resistance until some new stressor sends me into the state of exhaustion. From there I need a drink of the Living Water, often carried to me by the hands of loving friends. Renewed and replenished from the well that never runs dry, I am able to live abundantly, joyfully—even with the giant in the house.

CYNDI ZAHM SIEGFRIED and her husband Jim are co-founders of a support group for families facing catastrophic illnesses, f.a.i.t.H, (facing an illness through Him). They also speak on overcoming obstacles in marriage. Married for forty years, they have three daughters and sons-in-law, seven grandchildren and one very fat cat.

You show that you are a letter from Christ, the result of our ministry, written not with ink but with the Spirit of the living God, not on tablets of stone but on tablets of human hearts.

2 Corinthians 3:3

Hedge of Grace

Shonda Savage Whitworth

"Therefore, behold, I will hedge up her way with thorns, and I will build a wall against her so that she cannot find her paths " (Hosea 2:6 NASB).

"Lord, why am I lying here suffocating?" I asked as I lay bedridden, confined inside the four walls of my bedroom for six months. I felt like a child confined to my room. Breathing treatments awaited me every two hours to clear up my lungs. I felt like I received the death sentence. I knew I did something wrong, but I could not reason it out. "Lord, did I sin against You? Please show me; I want to be free."

Born a wild branch with the wayward name, Savage, I recognized a need for a Savior early in my life. I wanted salvation when I heard about the ever-burning fire of hell. I didn't like pain, and I certainly didn't want to live in affliction for eternity. The salvation message became clear right away with me at eleven years old because I wanted to avoid torture.

I despised my life growing up on the poor side of town with working parents. Even as a preteen, my parents expected me to clean house and prepare dinner for them and my younger brother. I dreamed of an exciting life.

My parents sent me to church every Sunday on the church bus. One summer, I attended a church girls' camp in the mountains. In the piney woods, I met Jesus. In that place I sensed His unconditional acceptance, something foreign to me. I became His loved one, a daughter of the living God (Romans 9:25-26).

I still had wild sap running through my veins as a wild branch grafted into the olive tree. So as a teenager, I refused to attend church. I pursued the life I desired, not the life others required of me. I escaped my parents' confinement to seek the pleasures that weren't allowed in my home. I couldn't live up to my parents' expectations. I counted the days until I could move out of my father's house.

When I finally moved out, I worked two jobs. Looking for a place to party, I wandered around in a nearby city one night. When I returned home the next day, I stopped at a convenience store. At the checkout, the clerk said, "I'm sorry to hear about your dad."

"What?" I questioned.

"Your dad died last night. You don't know?"

"No, I don't!" I ran out the door, and I cried all the way to the hospital. For several years my dad wrestled with cancer, but lost his battle on the night I chose to seek my own plans. I ignored my family through Dad's illness because I wanted to be free. I knew I disappointed my father, so I had to find another way to pursue my plans.

After Dad's death, my friends disappeared. So I joined the U.S. Air Force, hoping for an exotic assignment to chase my dreams. Then it happened. A good-looking cowboy two-stepped his way into my heart. My heart danced and sang tunes with his music. Eldon captured my attention with his ingenuity. But my commitment to the Air Force boot camp controlled my destiny. After my basic training, Eldon and I eloped and transferred to

Del Rio, Texas. There, I faced my first culture shock, not the adventurous assignment of my dreams.

Captured by my husband's good looks, I failed to communicate with him about his goals and dreams in life. I expected him to go along with whatever I wanted to do. But he had other plans. And I started to feel penned in again by my frustrations.

Trapped in South Texas with no way out, I sought another escape. I started my college education, but my first baby arrived. My classes left little time for my family. I earned a few credit hours before I eventually quit, focusing on my family. Again, my plans were frustrated.

I tried to run again, requesting transfers with the Air Force. But time and time again, my plans failed. And with each failed attempt, scratches from the thorns scarred my soul. I could not escape through the hedge of thorns, but I kept trying. Every direction I turned left me more spiritually and emotionally battered.

Finally, I shifted the blame of my failure to my husband. Stuck in a dead-end town with my dreams shattered, the seeds of resentment took root in the soil of my broken soul. Angry flames lashed out to those I loved the most—my family.

With all the obstructions, I decided to return to the place I met my Lord—in church. Though I returned to Christ, I longed for a way to escape to achieve my own way. I found a hole in the hedge as I attempted another way to fulfill my plans.

A mother of two at this point, I wanted to stay at home with my children. I despised leaving my infant in daycare. My heart cried louder than my baby cried when I left him in the arms of another. I signed up with work-at-home companies, but these programs did not work for me. The deficits were larger than the profits, eventually driving my family into a mountain of debt. Eldon disagreed with my plan to get rich quick through network marketing programs. Therefore, I blamed him for my failure. More resentment and bitterness grew from this failure. I worked for civil service five more years before paying off the debts that I ran up on the credit cards. My plans failed again.

Diagnosed with acute bronchitis, on the brink of pneumonia, I lay in bed for two months. Trapped within the walls of my bedroom, the Lord penned me up like a wild sheep.

Suffocating, I wished I had never been born. Self-pity controlled my thoughts. Because of my anger and verbal abuse, Eldon cautioned my friends who visited, "I have to warn you now, she's not herself."

Finally, I sought the Lord about my illness. I don't believe all illnesses come upon people due to sin. Job, a righteous man, experienced infliction.

Heaviness suffocated me. Trying to focus on ways to ease the pain, I wanted to hold my breath. But my efforts were fruitless.

"Lord, what is happening to me? If I've been so bad to deserve the death sentence, please take me now." He refused.

I woke up in between treatments with no energy to move, crying, "Lord, what have I done?"

In my quiet room inside my spirit I heard the still voice: *Stop blaming your husband. It's not his fault. I allowed you to go through all those situations. I wanted you to seek Me.*

All the scenes of my past played like movies in my mind, as if the Lord were walking me step-by-step. "Lord, I'm sorry I blamed Eldon. Please forgive me."

Peace and contentment poured over me as the strangling mucus loosened from my lungs. I felt truly free for the first time in my life, as I stopped seeking a way of escape and sought the One who sets us free.

His grace walled me in, so I could be protected, and I sought Him. I learned a wild branch can be tamed by His grace by abiding in the vine. Jesus said, "*I am the vine; you are the branches. If a man remains in me and I in him, he will bear much fruit; apart from me you can do nothing*" (John 15:5 NIV).

Now, I experience contentment more than ever. I belong to

God. Though I was prone to wander from Him, He promised to never leave me. By His grace, He frustrated my plans in order that I may turn to Him. After twenty years of marriage to the same man, one grown child and one child at home, I am so thankful for the Lord's hedge of grace in the circumstances that drew me closer to Him.

SHONDA SAVAGE WHITWORTH, speaker, writer, and teacher, encourages women through her personal experiences and the Word of God. Shonda and her husband, Eldon, live with their two sons in Del Rio, Texas. You can learn more about her ministry at http://www.EngraftedbyGrace.com and http://shondasjournal.blogspot.com.

That's the Cutest Kid

Penny Carlson

"Oh, God, why am I doing it all wrong? Where's Your grace, now when I need it the most?"

I can remember the first time I held him in my arms. It was love at first sight—and he wasn't even mine. Of course, he couldn't walk or talk yet, but it wasn't long before the cooing and smiling became hurtful words with later regrets. Why was this happening?

I've always had this amazing love and passion for kids—mine and everyone else's. Often I'm heard saying, "Oh my gosh, that's the cutest kid I've ever seen, if you ever need a babysitter call me!" Recently, I realized the power in those words.

It was the spring of 1993. I was at church. In the pew in front of me a Grandma was holding one of those "cutest little guys I'd ever seen." I informed Grandma I had fallen in love with her little bundle and I would love to baby-sit if ever needed.

September rolled around and I received a phone call. The woman on the other end of the line asked if I really meant what I'd said. I asked, "Who are you and what did I say?" She reminded me of the words I had spoken to her mother almost nine months ago. Her little boy, Derek, was now eighteen months old.

I explained that this was an expression I had always used and she was the first to take me up on my offer. "But," I told her, "I will think about it."

It had been a long time since I had done any babysitting. My own boys, Joshua and Dustin, were now in the fifth and sixth grade. As I hung up the phone that morning it hit me—my words had power. Wow! Suddenly, I knew this couldn't be something I simply tossed out every time I saw a cute kid.

That evening I shared with my husband, Alan, and my boys the thoughts I had of how I might stand behind those words. By offering childcare, I would be doing the *one* job I loved most and believed God had called me to do—being a mom! My family agreed this was the job for me, and it turned out to be a blessing for all involved.

We soon discovered Derek was three months premature when he was born weighing not quite two pounds. He was truly a miracle baby. His mom was a single mom and needed to go back to work. Grandma was not able to keep Derek full time, and there was no dad in the picture. God's grace entered into this situation. He already knew, even though I did not, that the words I'd spoken held the power to change the destiny of this precious child. As a family we would be able to invest in Derek's life. Joshua and Dustin were excited about having a little brother and even my husband seemed to like the idea. Alan had an opportunity to teach and train Derek from an early age just as he had done with our own two. Once again I had the chance to go out and purchase all the fun items necessary for a little one in our home.

Within a few months Derek became more than a child I babysat, eventually spending more time in our home than he did in his. Not only was Derek in our home during the day, he spent nights and weekends with us as well. Potty chairs, fingerprints on the walls, and rubber bath toys reminded me of the joys of my own two and those precious days gone by. I enjoyed watching our boys take on the "big brother" role, with one carrying Derek and the other the diaper bag. This was an unusual sight for a couple of teenage boys. He became so much a part of our family that when he wasn't with us we felt as if part of us had been left somewhere. By the time Derek was three, he was spending major holidays and going on vacation with us. Derek idolized his big brothers. Alan and I basically had a third child. I was in my prime again.

On the first day of Kindergarten, Derek had Grandma, Mom, and me to see him off. My days were scheduled with thoughts of treats for a party, helping out in the classroom, and chaperoning field trips to the pumpkin patch. I had always been very involved in those areas when my boys were young. I was usually the one mom on the block not ready for summer vacations or Christmas breaks to end. Because I had always been so involved in the lives of our boys and all their activities, I was enjoying this repeat season of my life.

As Derek continued to grow, his mom moved from place to place. His time spent with us turned into weekends, holidays, and summer vacations.

I still remember that Friday afternoon, walking into Derek's fourth grade class and introducing myself as Derek's Aunt. I'll never forget the look on Ms. Blames' face. "He's just another statistic," she bluntly said. My mother-anger rose up within me. She wasn't talking about just another statistic; she was talking about *my* child. How is it this child can barely write his first name let alone his last. Who's to blame? A single mom trying to survive—coming home too tired to deal with her child, or me, "the babysitter?" As I walked out of school that day with my arm around Derek's shoulder, I tried hard not to let my disappointment show. I knew it wasn't his fault.

I went home that evening, called my troops together, and shared my heart again concerning Derek's education and future. I felt it was time for a serious move on our part.

The smell of bacon and eggs seemed to hang heavy over the corner booth where I sat with Derek's mom that Monday morning. The thoughts in my heart were beating heavy in my chest, thoughts I now needed to share with Derek's mom. Slowly and carefully I shared the events that had taken place while she was out of town. I reminded her of my past concerns and her desire for her son's future.

As we talked, it was evident we all wanted the very best for Derek. However, the next step would be hard. I knew some serious changes needed to take place, or Derek stood a good chance of going down the wrong path. The statistics concerning minorities and low-income, single parent, families were true for the most part. I also knew Derek was in our life for a reason. He would not become what his teacher had spoken (not if I had anything to do with it.) So summoning all my courage I simply said, "If you can't give this child what he needs to help assure him of a different path than his father's—please let us help." And with that Derek's mom wrote a statement on a piece of typing paper and signed it. She had it notarized and Alan and I became joint custodians of Derek.

I don't think it was because she didn't love him, but more because she felt we could give him so much more. Funny thing is, even though we loved Derek as much as we loved our own two boys, it wasn't enough. The older he got, the more evident it became. We could not give him the one thing he desired more than anything else—his own mother's love! He began to see her choice as a lack of love, even abandonment.

As a mom, I can look back on choices I've made with my own two. I know it was always my heart's desire to give them the very best. I knew my intentions were pure. But things didn't always turn out the way I had intended and often pain was created.

Why is it on those days when I try to walk using God's grace, it turns out to be anything but grace? In fact, many times I know

I haven't extended the same grace to Derek that God has extended to me.

Tonight, as I sit here on the side of Derek's bed gently stroking his afro curls, he looks so peaceful. Yet in his heart I know there is great pain and it hurts me so. Those days when he struggles to explain his identity to his peers, or when the assignment in English is to write about *his* family tree, I know his heart aches. I sense the awkwardness in his voice when he tries to explain how he has two big brothers and yet calls us Uncle Alan and Aunt Penny instead of Mom and Dad.

As I gently kiss him on the forehead, I'm reminded of the uniqueness of our situation. Derek has been with us 98 percent of his life. Even though his mother would never allow us to officially adopt Derek, as much as we would have loved to, we are still family! And even though we are not blood related, we are bound by the blood of Jesus and the love of God. With His grace we will continue to help Derek realize how valuable and precious he is to the One who created him.

Yes, there are struggles, as with any family. But it's the hug after school with a smile and the usual question, "So Aunt Penny, how was your day?" that reminds me the words I speak today hold just as much power as the ones I spoke over thirteen years ago. And God's grace is sufficient for Derek, his mom, and for me when words are not enough.

Oh, and by the way, he is *still* the cutest kid!

God has given PENNY CARLSON a passion for her kids and everyone else's. There's not enough pages in this book to brag on Alan, her awesome husband of thirty-three years, or their amazing sons, Joshua, Dustin, and Derek. And of course Howard the Bassett Hound must be mentioned. They reside in Scottsdale, Arizona.

"Take a Risk!"

Jan Edith Taylor

It was the summer of 1986 and we were visiting my sister's in-laws at their cottage on Dewey Lake in the Irish Hills of Michigan. Sunday morning everyone was sleeping soundly when I reached for my Bible and headed down the street to a tree stump I had spotted near the lake.

As I sat down, the tranquility that settled around me was ample reward for this moment of seeking God's presence and direction.

The sun emerged over the lake above the eastern ridge of trees and shrubbery, mirrored in the surface of the water. The freshwater ripples caught the sunlight with blinding intensity and I could smell the humid promise of another hot summer day.

I soaked in the peace of birds singing and the gentle lap of waves on the beach as I read and meditated on the devotional for the day. Now, ready to start my day, I climbed the slope back to the road.

Suddenly my random thoughts were interrupted by a question that entered my mind: *"Are you willing to take a risk?"*

After a moment of hesitation, I realized this must be God's voice. I reasoned, "If it is God, then it's okay to take a risk."

The next impression was equally clear: *"Buy a cottage now!"*

Owning a cottage in the Irish Hills was a dream of mine from childhood. I can remember so many weekends when our family drove to a public area in the gently rolling countryside to spend the day near one of the lakes. Inevitably, sometime during the day we viewed places for sale, and wished one of them was ours.

After I married and our family moved back to Michigan, we often looked at lake property, but it seemed a like an impossible dream.

Now on this Sunday morning I returned to our friends' cottage with many practical objections running through my head. After all, our son was a junior in high school and our daughter a freshman in a private college, and we had no savings. My husband and I had good jobs, but with the expense of a daughter in undergraduate school, we were thankful each semester when there was enough money in the bank to pay the bills.

However, the confirmation of God's command came on the ride home when my husband, Ed, casually shared, "You know, this morning I went down by the lake to have some quiet time, and I believe God told me we should buy a cottage."

Hardly able to restrain my excitement, I told Ed and our son, Bill, of my own experience. The rest of the trip home we discussed how we could take the first step financially to do this. By the time we arrived home, we were convinced. If we could sell the wheat land my husband had inherited from his grandfather in Oklahoma, we could, indeed, buy a place on the lake. The arrangements seemed to be falling neatly into place. In our exhilaration I had forgotten the test of faith implied in the question: *"Are you willing to take a risk?"*

During our weekend at the lake we saw a cottage for sale. Now serious in our intentions, we made a quick inventory of how much we could afford and what we would need, including the extra luxury of a boat so Bill could water ski with his friends. Then we called the telephone number on the real estate sign to set up a time to see the cottage.

When we saw inside, it was everything on our wish list, including the price. Bill was ecstatic when the owners also agreed to include a speed boat in the mortgage. They were eager for us to sign on the dotted line, but we told them we had to straighten out details for the sale of Ed's inheritance first. We would be in touch with them in the days ahead.

Over the months that followed we were able to straighten out the title to the land, but after putting it up for sale, nothing happened. Meanwhile the owners of the cottage called a couple of times but when we did not move forward with our plans, we didn't hear from them anymore.

One weekend our hopes were crushed when we saw a sign marked "sold" on the property. My husband and I were puzzled. "Why had God given us such clear direction and then not allowed the wheat land to sell?" Secretly, my husband and I were discouraged and felt that God had let us down. Our son, Bill, was especially disillusioned and refused to talk about the entire affair. The demands of work and daily responsibilities closed in and our hope of owning a cottage was pushed into the background.

Two years later Ed and I took a wedding anniversary trip to Germany. As we sat on a private balcony, relaxing after a cheese and wine dinner against the backdrop of snowcapped ridges in the Alps, my husband and I finally had the courage to talk about our disappointment over the hope to own a cottage. It was not a question of doubting that God had clearly told us to buy a cottage. Neither of us doubted that. So what happened? Why didn't things fall into place?

Eventually as we talked, the truth dawned on us. Out of His abundant love for us, God had chosen to give us the desire of our hearts, a cottage on Dewey Lake. However, He had asked,

"Are you willing to take a risk?"

I had said, "Yes," but when tested, I chose to rely on the sale of Ed's inheritance and when the land did not sell, my confidence in God's provision faltered and we refused to go any further.

We had lost our blessing! Was it too late? Would God still act on our behalf if we were willing to trust Him now, even when the situation continued to look impossible?

We decided that we would step out in faith to see if, in His patient love, God would give us a second chance. We resolved when we returned home to walk through every door that He opened.

Back in Michigan, reality set in. As the first weekend drew near, I thought to myself, "What were we thinking?" We now had *two* children in private colleges and were fiscally stretched to the limit! I voiced my feelings to Ed, and he, too, had second thoughts.

Then on Friday the phone rang. It was my sister. She informed me, "My in-laws' cottage on Dewey Lake is vacant this weekend and I wondered if you and Ed wanted to use it?"

With a sense of awe, I placed my hand over the phone to tell Ed about the offer. As we looked at each other, we both recognized the unmistakable message: "It's time to see if the first door will open."

Next day when we arrived at the lake, just down the street was a cottage for sale. Surrounded by attractive decks on three sides, tubs of flowers overflowing in the yard and on the porches, its large windows looked from the hillside onto the lake. I called the realtor.

Within an hour we were able to see the cottage and although it was small, the inside was as charming as the outside. The price was more than we had planned, but included in the cost was a sizable tract of land behind the cottages up and down the road. The realtor assured us that this land could be sold to these landowners. Once the down payment was made, she encouraged, the money from the sale of the extra land could be applied to our principal to bring down the monthly payments. Would this really happen? I asked my sister and she warned me: her in-laws thought the land was worthless. "No one wants that land," they cautioned us. "You shouldn't count on selling it."

In our hearts was God's crucial question, "Are you willing to take a risk?" Who was right? What would we do?

After our previous failure to trust God, we decided to believe our realtor. We worked out all of the finances and the owner accepted our offer.

The day came! We signed the papers and the picturesque little lake house was ours. We had trusted in God's goodness and His ability to provide. Not only had our walk of faith allowed God to bless my husband and me, but the first night Bill came with some college friends, complete with sleeping bags, to officially claim the fulfillment of his dreams.

Meanwhile, the word went out that we were selling the land behind the cottages, and the land sold like hot cakes. But that was not the end of it. Soon after we bought our place on Dewey Lake, the land Ed had inherited also sold!

In 2001 my husband and I retired, added on to the "cottage," and moved there making it our permanent home. As a family we are still filled with wonder of how God gave us this beautiful place on the water, with gracious neighbors, and a ministry of healing to all who come to this special spot for the blessing of peace it gives.

What would have happened if we had not acted on the command God gave us is difficult to imagine now. Nevertheless, the lesson is clear to all with whom we have shared this story: God delights to bless His people, but our part is to place our trust totally in His grace and when God directs, be willing to "Take a risk!"

JAN TAYLOR delights in writing and collecting personal stories that reveal the character of God. Jan enjoys gardening and travel, especially when it includes visits to her children and two grandsons who live in Washington, DC. Jan and her husband, Ed, reside in Brooklyn, Michigan.

The Perfect Mom for Cooper

Kay Klebba

I slumped in the doctor's office chair. "Your son exhibits the symptoms of Aspberger's Syndrome," the doctor said. "It's a form of autism." While she danced around the words, careful only to say he had the symptoms, I tried to remember what I had read about this confusing, multi-faceted syndrome. Did kids with Aspberger's function at a high level, or were they the children who rocked silently in corners? I searched my memory while she casually knocked my world off its axis. "Cooper is very highly functioning," the doctor told me as she picked hairs off her sleeve. I wanted to scream and shake her, but I sat and said nothing.

Questions scattered through my mind. Does she mean that Coop will never be normal? What is normal anyway? Why do I have a child with autism? Why would God give me this child when I was clearly not ready for him?

For months we suspected something was wrong with Cooper, so we started him in speech and occupational therapy. Twice a week for seven weeks I piled all four kids in the hot van for the forty-five mile trip to the therapist. Tired, frustrated, and overwhelmed, I now faced the ugly truth.

Will Cooper ever want to play with the neighborhood kids? Will Cooper ever have a friend when he can't reach out? How will he communicate when his little world is black and white and the English language is shaded gray?

It wasn't fair. I didn't ask for four children including a set of twins, but I'd rolled with the punches and kept smiling. I loved them, watched over them, and prayed for them. All I wanted was normal children.

But Cooper had Aspberger's Syndrome along with developmental delays. There was no cure, no known cause. Over the next few weeks, I struggled to control my emotions. As a mother, I felt disheartened. As a follower of God, I felt angry. Why would God do this to me? To my family. To my child. Could someone please tell me how God was taking care of this mother of four? Was I some cosmic joke to Him?

All of my children would be affected by Cooper's problem. Was the situation fair to them or to Cooper? Stumbling, swearing, and just about cursing God, I found no answers and put away my Bible in disgust.

A few weeks later the phone rang. "God put it on my heart to call you," said my sister, Dawn. She asked how I felt, and I opened the vault. I cried and yelled and cried some more. When I was spent and exhausted, Dawn quieted my heart, "God knows you are angry, and this is not about you."

"What do you mean this isn't about me?" I said. "This has everything to do with me and how Cooper's autism affects my family. I have to change our meals, our schedules, and everything about our daily lives. How in the world is this not about me?"

Dawn answered with God's truth. "This is about God giving Cooper the perfect mom for him," she said with love. "God knows you will stand up for Coop and fight for him. You'll care for him, and Cooper will become the best Cooper possible because of you." She paused and added, "You are the perfect mom for Cooper."

Dawn was right. At that moment, I felt God's undeserved grace wash over me, filling me with strength. I couldn't focus on me; I had to focus on Cooper. I would be his protector, the one who let him explore and expand. I would be his advocate in countless school meetings and doctor appointments. When I didn't have the strength to go on, I would open my Bible and pray. I'm not a perfect mom and never will be, but I could be a pretty good mom for all my kids, especially Coop.

I still struggle with my son's autism. I battle to accept who Cooper is and what he can do without limiting or overprotecting him. I cry when I make Cooper study his spelling words one more time, because he spells words according to their sounds rather than the dictionary. I rejoice when he gets a 100 percent on the same test he took last week. If a new treatment doesn't work, I try something else. I can never cure Cooper, but I help him start the day calmer and handle situations differently. My son is funny and wonderful, and I laugh at all the "Cooperisms" that come from his mouth.

Yes, motherhood isn't about me. It's about God giving a mother to four wonderful children including one who stands out and demands a little more work. I am God's gift to Cooper, the perfect mom for a unique child. And he is God's gift to me.

KAY KLEBBA, the mother of four incredible children, is happily married to Scott. Kay's passion is speaking and writing to women about the hilarity of their blessings. Please visit her blog at http://kayklebba.blogspot.com or email her at kayklebba@gmail.com.

His Longings Linger

Lesli Westfall

Longings… That one word alone can describe the intense feelings I have felt desiring children of my own or may describe one who is searching for more out of his or her life. But what happens when one does not have any longings or a God-intended purpose? Or has a baby to fill their empty arms? Better yet, what happens when the God-intended purpose, the well-watered garden of the soul has become a dry, barren land?

I had it all, a wonderful life. However, some days I crashed, days where I felt such a sense of hopelessness. Crying out to God in prayer, I asked Him for His purpose for my life. I searched *on my own* to fill the void, a place that only God can fill, through the act of busyness. My pursuits only led to temporary fulfillment with empty hands and a depleted heart, standing upon barren land.

At a Mother's Day church service the minister spoke on various aspects of barrenness in people's lives. He spoke on women desiring children. There was a stirring in me, a rapid beat of my heart, a weakness in my knees and a well of tears in my eyes—an all too familiar feeling. I liken it to the day I was born again.

In most Mother's Day church services, mothers are asked to stand to be recognized and are given a single rose. In this service it was as if I entered into the Master's Garden. He did not hand me only one rose, but placed a beautiful bouquet in my hands! A bouquet of His desires, His intended purpose for my life: motherhood. It was a perfect bouquet, nothing out of place, beautiful and refreshing. My husband and I walked out of the church passing through the portico of columns, the sun of an early Texas summer day shining on us. The morning sun was not only shining on my face, but the Son had also shone brightly in my heart. I thought to myself, "Great! I'll have a family soon!" In my hands were the longings, an answer to my prayer, and a hint of fragrance from His garden.

Many days and months passed. The emotions of feeling forsaken and unfruitful due to infertility caused the roses, which represented my desire for motherhood, to wilt. Barrenness became like years of drought, my empty womb had taken its toll on the bouquet of my longings, and they became dry and brittle. No amount of my tears could replenish the suppleness of the tender leaves or the soft petals.

When a rose loses its vibrancy, the thorns always remain. They are protruding, sharp, and numerous as ever before. When the longings are not fulfilled in time, "our time," like in my case, if one is not careful, the thorns will tend to prick, just like the long years of awaiting a child. There is not only one thorn on a stem, but many thorns. Those many thorns were the distress of numerous trials for me, a prickling of my heart producing a better character in me. A thorn of bitterness: Was I going to be bitter at my friend who was expecting after trying to conceive for a very short time? Or was I going to be a blessing to the creation God placed in her womb?

The thorn of endless questions: "Are you married?"

Gladly I replied, "Yes, nineteen years!"

"Wow!" they'd say. "How many children do you have?"

I'd say, "Uh, we do not have any children yet."

They would respond, "Well, do you *want* children?"

By now, internally I would be rolling my eyes into the back of my head! My standard reply along with a smile would be, "Yes, I believe they will come soon!" However, the thought of that word *soon* was just a word that had no definition to me, a word without a defining moment but a definite feeling of hopelessness. Ouch! The prick of another thorn, becoming the prick of the needle searching for answers to the cause of my barren womb.

Then the deepest prickle of all, the news from medical experts in the field saying, "Your clinical history and age are against you." The thorn of unexplained infertility.

Over the years the sweet scent of the roses, my desire to become a mother, became a musty smell, a stench of unfulfilled expectations and disappointments. For a season, I had tossed the spray of roses, the longings, and the dream away. I did not want them anymore; it hurt too badly. Even though the Master Gardener had pruned my heart through the prickling of the thorns, the scars were just freshly healed.

The Song of Solomon 4:16 (NASB) says, "*Awake O north wind and come in wind of the south; Make my garden breathe out fragrance, Let its spices be wafted abroad. May my beloved come into his garden and eat its choice fruits.*" What had not occurred to me is that the Master Gardener was trying to rush currents of air into my heart. He was trying to stir up that desire for motherhood again. Still, the atmosphere of my heart was … *still*. However, He has a way of arousing our senses, our broken dreams and our lost desires, He changes not.

One day at the home of another dear friend, she told me she was expecting again, all of a sudden it was as if I caught a whiff of the fragrance of the roses! The scent re-awakened the longings God had placed there so many years past. Like coffee brewing and biscuits baking, like the smell of freshly mown grass … the fragrance of the roses, the desire for motherhood became pungent again. Wafting up from His heavenly Garden into the depths of my heart, so much so that I excused myself from my friend's presence and went into her bathroom and silently sobbed.

A Chinese proverb says, "A bit of fragrance always lingers from the hand that gives you roses." His longings had been lingering in my heart without my awareness. As much as I tried to toss the bouquet, as many times as I had tried to crush and grind the petals to make potpourri… they still lingered. I sat in her bathroom and remembered the Word, *All my longings lie open before You, my sighing is not hidden from You.* I left there with a fragrance and opened my arms to receive again that beautiful bouquet, the God-intended purpose for my life.

Never again did I toss my spray of roses. I have kept my longings for motherhood before Him. I began to replenish the bouquet's life source with the Living Water, watering my heart with daily reading of His Word. There is so much nourishment in that Living Water! In each drop, there is hope! There is healing for a broken heart! There is a sense of purpose that His plans are good for me, with a *final outcome*! There is a promise of a perfecting that which is concerning me, perfecting our lingering longings!

As this God-given desire, this ever-living bouquet was resplendent in all of its color and fragrance daily, I just could not keep the roses to myself! I wanted to hand out my bouquet to other women as Lisa Bevere says to "lend voice to their lingering longings," their desire for motherhood. I had been taught that it is more blessed to give than to receive, that the seeds that I plant in other lives would produce a harvest in my own life.

The Master Gardener provided a fertile field of barren women, a Christian infertility support group, for me to lead. A field to sow into lives, one beautiful rose after another. One rose, would be a hand-made baby blanket attaching itself as a symbol of hope to hold onto to for an empty womb. Another rose was a shoulder to cry on, soft and comforting petals to the tear-stained cheek. And then there was another rose, one with a long, strong stem. This rose symbolized a prayer of faith for a fellow sister grieving over a miscarriage, the loss of life, the loss of yet another desire unfulfilled.

The roses that I have given away are unique because God has prepared them perfectly for the intended soul. Just as a florist prepares a bouquet of roses for the receiver by stripping the stems of the prickly thorns, so are my roses. My bouquet was stripped of the thorns that I was giving away. He has taken away the prickling of the pain and suffering. You see, the thorns of my roses, He wore as a woven crown upon His head as he hung on the cross.

Just as the verse in the Song of Solomon says, Can you feel the awakening of the north and the south winds stirring those long lost dreams and longings of your heart?

Are you beginning to smell the fragrance coming from His Garden? He is inviting you to enter. Step onto fertile ground into the garden, reach up to His nail-scarred hands and gather *in your hands*, the desires, and the God-intended purpose for your life. Gather in your bosom the bouquet of your longings again.

LESLI WESTFALL encourages women in the love and Word of God as she leads Hearts Of Promise and Expectation (H.O.P.E.), a Christian infertility support group in Houston, Texas. Her passions are family and friends, teaching children etiquette and travel. She enjoys life with her man of faith, live-in comedian and best friend, Larry. Contact her at: hope@lakewood.cc.

Talkin' to Jesus

Michael S. Tarrant

"Michael, please don't let anything else happen to Lauren."

Tears pooled in my wife's eyes as she whispered the plea in my ear. We stood holding each other, framed in the doorway of a hospital room while our daughter, a Clemson University senior, lay gravely injured in the bed behind us.

"I won't. I promise," I whispered back to Karin. Reluctantly, I released her and watched as she quietly walked out, leaving me to look after Lauren for the night.

The previous twenty-four hours had been every parent's worst nightmare. A driver's momentary inattentiveness forever altered the course of our daughter's life, and our own lives as well. With multiple severe injuries and massive bone loss in her leg, amputation seemed unavoidable.

Alone with my daughter, I sat down in the straight-backed chair by Lauren's bed and stroked her cheek. She blinked open one eye.

"Daddy," she said drifting in and out of drug-induced sleep, "I'm really glad you're here."

"Me, too, Chicken Little," I answered. "Me, too."

A half hour later I got up, went over to a convertible cot that would be my bed and laid back. I wasn't brave enough to close my eyes. The darkened room flickered with unfamiliar lights while strange sounds clicked and whirred. Beyond the door, an undercurrent of constant activity added to the surreal environment—nurses walking briskly, their voices sometimes carrying into the room, ubiquitous visitors talking and laughing too loudly.

Did this hospital have visiting hours at all, or was it just a popular nightspot for folks in the upstate? Well, whatever, I reflected. Rather than feeling annoyed, I was actually thankful for the distraction.

Abruptly, without warning my thoughts took a more sinister turn.

I let this happen. I allowed, even encouraged, Lauren to buy the moped that may ultimately destroy her. Karin begged me not to go along with it, but I hadn't backed her.

"Knock it off!" I whispered aloud to myself. "That kind of thinking won't help Lauren, or anybody now. Just close your eyes and go to sleep."

But closing my eyes meant being alone with my imagination. And though I had no clear concept of what happened on that street in Clemson the night before, fleeting thoughts of what Lauren must have endured ran through my mind. Still, the cleansing light of day, and a mind and body not yet overcome by fatigue, had given me the strength to will those images away.

But now, unable to keep my eyes open any longer, a scene began playing in my head like a movie. I could see Lauren on her moped, coming down that busy, rain-slick street, the car turning in front of her. I felt her panic when she realized there was no way to avoid a collision. I saw her fragile little frame hitting the cold rigid steel of the car, the moped spinning and grinding into the pavement...

Enough! The imagery was too excruciating.

In desperation, as a last resort, I began to pray.

Lord, I'm not ready to deal with what happened to my child. I don't want my mind to take me there. A time will come when I'll have to find a way to deal with this, but I can't let this sap my strength now. I need to be a hundred percent so that I can best help her. Please take this image out of my mind. My child has such strength through her faith in You. Please grant me that same strength. Please grant me Your peace that surpasses all understanding.

I opened my eyes. To my amazement, the vivid, torturous imaginings ceased. Instead, my thoughts carried me back in time to my own childhood. I was six years old, standing barefoot and shirtless in the simmering heat of the backyard at the house where I grew up.

We lived on Reynolds Pond Road, about eight miles out of Aiken, right near the forty-acre Reynolds Pond. An immense swamp flowed east from the pond, enclosing both sides of Shaw's Creek until the swamp and the creek merged into the Spanish-moss-canopied Edisto River, the longest black water river in the world. Our house stood on sandy earth, amidst pine trees, cedars, and Carolina cherries. It was the first high ground beyond the tupelos that are rooted in the muck of the swamp. On summer afternoons, many a wayward rattlesnake, cottonmouth, or copperhead slithered off course into our yard.

In our young years, my older brother, Bobby, and I had already been the consistent victors in countless battles with snakes. Deadly with a BB gun, Bobby had been known to pump as many as 200 BB's into a single snake. He was also handy with a hoe, yet savvy enough to know when it was safe to take on a snake by himself and when to call in reinforcements.

Our reinforcement was Becky. I guess in today's vernacular Becky would be a housekeeper or a nanny, but back then we didn't know that. Becky was black, but we didn't know that, either. All we knew was Becky was almost always at our house, especially when Mama was sick. She had cancer. We also knew

Becky took care of us, and she loved us, and we loved her, too.

On this particular afternoon, Bobby and I were out in the sand pile between the house and the well house—a shed with a brick foundation which housed the pump. It was also where we parked our bicycles and kept our red, green, and blue metal John Deere toys.

A rustle in the pine straw next to the sand pile caused Bobby and me to look up from our dump trucks. A big water moccasin was holding its shovel-shaped head above its thick body, flicking its forked tongue in survey of its surroundings. Recognizing this snake was not to be fought by two little boys like us, we ran to the house for Becky.

"Becky, there's a big ole snake in the backyard!" Bobby yelled as we slammed through the back porch door. "I think it's a cottonmouth!"

Becky stood no more than four feet tall, her hair always pulled back tightly in a knot. She wore a white apron over skirts that almost touched the floor, and sturdy white leather shoes like the kind nurses wore in those days. Despite her diminutive size and cumbersome clothes, she could move with lightning speed to rescue little boys when in danger. Becky was out the back porch door in a split second, with Bobby and me right behind.

Apparently, the snake sensed the commotion and its impending doom and made a beeline for any potential sanctuary the well house might offer. In hot pursuit, Becky grabbed the hoe kept at the ready beside the back door during the months when snakes were active. But the water moccasin had too much of a lead, and finding a broken brick in the foundation, slithered out of sight under the well house. Undaunted, Becky quickly set up surveillance.

"Bobby, you stay right here on this side of the well house. Michael, you go round to the back where you can see, but don't you get too close. You chirren watch underneath, and if that snake comes crawlin' out, you holler. I'm goin' to boil some water. We're go'ne boil that snake out from under that well house."

I ran to my designated spot, keeping a healthy distance from the well house, with one eye on the back foundation and the other on my brother who had retrieved his BB gun and stood stock still, staring at the front of the little white shed. No sign of the snake.

Before long, Becky came out the back door in a trot, carrying the kettle from the stove. Steam conspicuously spewed from the spout even in the withering afternoon heat. She ran to the hole in the foundation that the snake had crawled down and emptied the boiling kettle into the crevice. To my utter horror, within seconds the water moccasin shot out of a previously unnoticed crack on my side of the well house. It sped right at me, its huge mouth wide open and whiter inside than the freshly laundered sheets hanging motionlessly on the clothesline.

"Here it comes!" I shrieked. Before I could break into a run in the opposite direction, Becky's hoe swung down like a guillotine, decapitating the monster in one swift, deadly stroke.

The severed body of the serpent lay writhing at our feet while Becky walked out into the field and dug a hole. She came back and picked up the remains, which coiled around the hoe like a kudzu vine. Then she placed the carcass in the hole and covered it with the sandy soil.

"Ya'll boys stay away from that snake now, 'cause you know a snake don't die 'til sundown," she called as she placed the hoe against the house and disappeared onto the back porch to resume the daily chores.

Becky was not only our protector, but a one-of-a-kind teacher as well. We learned some of life's most important lessons from her. She was brave, fast, and knew how to handle herself amidst the challenges of life in rural South Carolina. Best of all, she was a champion of small boy's causes.

But her most awe-inspiring ability was a simple part of her daily routine. Late in the afternoons, when the heat of the day was just beginning to abate, she would set up her ironing board at one end of the kitchen where the breeze from the front of the house would flow all the way through to the back. There, while she ironed, she talked.

"Yes, Jesus," she'd say. Then she'd utter a few sentences that couldn't quite be heard, then, "No, Jesus." This apparently one-sided conversation continued for as long as there was ironing to be done. I'd sometimes play on the floor and try to listen in, but I could never quite make out the topic of the conversations.

Finally, one day, curiosity overwhelmed me. "Becky, who you talkin' to?"

"I'm talkin' to Jesus, chile."

"Does He hear you?"

"He sho do."

"But how do you know? Does He answer you back?"

"He do. Sometimes He answers me right back. And sometimes He don't answer for a while, but He always answers."

I hadn't understood her answer at the time. I think I even thought that for all her outstanding virtues, Becky was a little delirious by late afternoon after chasing two boys and keeping up the house and helping Mama all day. Sane people knew that the only time you talked to Jesus was right before you went to bed, or had a big meal, or if you were in Sunday School or church.

But this night, lying on a cot in that hospital room, with my own child lying helpless and hurt a few feet away, I thought of Becky.

I talked to Jesus, too.

And at last I began to understand.

You then, my son, be strong in the grace that is in Christ Jesus (2 Timothy 2:1 NIV).

A native of the Sand Hills of South Carolina, MICHAEL SMITH TARRANT has over thirty years experience in finance, organizational effectiveness, and business facilitation for numerous Fortune 500 companies across the country. But Michael's real passion is his family, and writing and speaking about amazing true stories of God's infinite, incredible love. Contact him at kamitar@bellsouth.net.

Mentors

Get Published Now 2008 Team

Ron Benson is a husband, father, writer, and pastor. Ron has been published in *Light and Life*, *Wittenburg Door*, *Bible Advocate*, *Discipleship Journal*, *Leadership Journal*, and *Today's Christian*. In addition, Ron is a regular contributor to *Plain Truth Magazine*. As a "P.K." (Preacher's Kid), Ron spent the majority of his life within spitting distance of a church, so he knows how to take careful aim at the church without being careless. His satire pieces are designed to prompt laughter, promote good thinking, and instigate change. Ron's book, *Coach's Challenge: Faith, Football, and Filling the Father Gap*, a collaboration with ESPN football analyst Mike Gottfried, was published by Howard Publishing in September 2007. GPN Mentor of Daphne Delay and Carol Jones.

Caroline Coleman has degrees from Princeton University, Christ Church, Oxford University, and Columbia Law School. She clerked for a federal district judge and worked as a litigation associate at Davis Polk & Wardwell, before "retiring" from the practice of law to take care of her children and write fiction. She sold her first novel, *Loving Soren*, to Broadman & Holman after pitching it at the 2002 Glorieta conference. *Writer's Digest* recently published two of her articles on writing fiction. She lives in New York City with her two children. She has been on faculty at Glorieta in 2005 and 2007. GPN Mentor of Ally Johnson and Rebecca Dowden.

Cheri Cowell, an accomplished speaker and author with over 100 articles in such magazines as *Marriage Partnership* and *Light and Life*, and her stories appear in over ten anthologies including *Chicken Soup for the Grandma's Soul*. Cheri says of her opportunity to teach once again at Glorieta, "Through teaching I am able to not only give back what I've been so generously given, but also to encourage others to share their own gifts and passions." Her new book *Direction: Discernment for the Decisions of Your Life* was released in December 2007. GPN Mentor of Penny Carlson and Michael Tarrant.

Linda Gilden knows the tremendous impact and power of words and loves helping new writers discover the joy in choosing just the right ones. She is the author of the *Love Notes* series (New Hope). *Mommy Pick-Me-Ups* (New Hope) was released in April 2008. Linda Gilden has written and ghostwritten many other books and hundreds of articles appearing in *Focus on the Family, Focus on Your Child, HomeLife, Family Fun, The Lookout, Discipleship Journal, Writers Digest*, and others. She is a freelance editor for several publishers and teaches regularly at national writers' conferences. Linda leads a writing group and is managing editor of *The Encourager*, a monthly magazine of First Baptist Spartanburg (SC). Linda's husband is her head cheerleader. Her three children can often be seen rolling their eyes and saying, "There she goes again. She's going to write about this!" Linda is the Editorial Director of Get Published Now.

Get Published Now 2008 Team

Doreen Hanna authored the biblically based rite-of-passage program, *Becoming a Modern Day Princess*. She has been a contributing writer for various compilation books. As a faculty member and speaker for CLASServices she passionately encourages women of all ages to experience the joy and abundance in a relationship with Christ. GPN Mentor of Cheryl Dore and Jan Taylor.

Lessie Harvey has a passion for teaching, speaking, and writing. She loves encouraging and coaching writers and speakers as they give birth to the dreams and desires of their hearts. Lessie is a leader in Bible Study Fellowship International, an active member in her church, a personality trainer, a speaker, and a published author. GPN Mentor of Nancy Biffle and Leslie Westfall.

Gus Henne has a personal mission: *Helping Others Tell Their Stories*. With over twenty-five years of printing, publishing, and marketing experience, Gus has helped over 380 writers get into print. Gus is always ready to answer a question or share an idea for your book project. His two areas of expertise are marketing books through non-traditional channels and anthologies. He is the publisher of the Get Published Now project at Glorieta. You can reach him at www.foreverbooks.ca.

Karen Jordan, MA, Professional and Technical Writing, serves as an adjunct writing instructor at the University of Arkansas at Little Rock and as a Teacher-Consultant for the Little Rock Writing Project. Karen also assists other writers as freelance editor and in her writing workshops—*BLESSED: Building Legacies. Encouraging Spiritual Stories. Equipping Disciples.* As a writer, teacher, speaker, and CLASS graduate, Karen addresses topics about her faith and writing. In addition to her contributions to books, periodicals, academic publications, and e-zines, Karen also publishes her own blog and Web site at www.karenjordan.net.

Karen and her husband, Dan, live in Sherwood, Arkansas—they have two married children and six grandchildren. GPN Mentor of Shonda Whitworth and Ruby Heaton.

Allison Pittman is the author of *With Endless Sight*, the third novel in her Crossroads of Grace series, as well as the memoir *Saturdays With Stella*—a book devoted to sharing the lessons she learned when she took her beloved Stella through a doggy obedience class. She serves as co-president of the Christian Writers Group in San Antonio where she lives with her husband, Mike, and their three sons. GPN Mentor of Michelle Bengstson and Pam Morrison.

Karen Porter is a national retreat and seminar speaker, the author/co-author of six books, and a successful businesswoman. Her newest book project, released by Random House/Multnomah publishers, is: *I'll Bring the Chocolate: Satisfying a Woman's Cravings for Friendship and Faith*. Karen is a frequent guest on regional and national radio and TV programs. She contributes to national magazines such as *Focus on the Family*, *Discipleship Journal*, and *American Taste*. She has also written curriculum for *Lifeway Resources*. Karen founded **kae creative solutions** a communications consulting firm.

Karen says her marriage to George is her greatest achievement, but she'd love to talk to you about her five grandchildren! Karen's favorite activity is continuing her life-long quest for the perfect purse. Karen is a people person, plain and simple, and you are going to love to laugh with her and maybe even cry a little as she shares her joys and struggles. GPN Mentor of Linda Mitchell and Susan Norris.

Donna Savage knew little about the freelance writing business when she registered for GCWC in 2005. Since then, she's sold articles to magazines like *Today's Christian Woman*,

Discipleship Journal, Pray!, Marriage Partnership, FullFill, The Upper Room, and *Deacon.* Donna also contributed to *Women Ask, Women Answer* (Thomas Nelson, 2008), *Chicken Soup for the Empty Nester's Soul* (2008), and *Chicken Soup Celebrating Mothers and Daughters* (2007). A pastor's wife in Las Vegas for twenty-five years, Donna is still learning how to juggle time for writing with her church ministry commitments, speaking/teaching schedule, and family life. She taught her first writing workshop at Florence Littauer's kitchen table. GPN Mentor of Linda Davis and Kay Klebba.

Pamela Sonnemoser is a speaker, author, and certified personality trainer. She is on the training faculty with CLASServices. Pamela is the 2008 recipient of the YWCA Woman of Excellence Award for Emerging Women Leaders in Northwest Missouri. For information about Pamela's speaking ministry go to www.pamelasonnenmoser.com. GPN Mentor of Ruth Holland and Ginger O'Neill.

Carol Stratton has written articles for the *Grand Rapids Press, Zionsville Times Sentinel, Purpose, Christian Communicator, In Touch, Fandangle Forsyth Women, Women's Touch* magazines and has reviewed books for the Christian book preview Web site. She has taught at Write On—Southern Indiana's Writers' conference, has been on Moody's Midday Connection radio program and is a judge for the International Tweeners Ministries Book Contest. Currently she is working on a middle grade novel and a picture book.

A mother of four grown children, she and her husband live in the Chicago area. Because she has moved a lot during her life, she has developed a Web site, www.ChangingZipCodes.com to encourage those who find themselves relocating. She is available to speak to groups on Being That Friend You Always Wanted,

Becoming Barnabas, and Developing a Welcome Mat ministry in Your Church. You can contact her at carolstrat@yahoo.com. GPN Mentor of Anita Brooks and Cyndi Siegfried.

Lee Warren is an author, editor, and freelance writer with three books and more than 300 articles in print. He writes for *Baptist Press Sports*, is the former singles columnist for *Christianity Today Online*, and the former sports columnist for his local Christian newspaper. His books include *Single Servings: 90 Devotions to Feed Your Soul* and *The Experience of Christmas: Family Devotions & Activities to Prepare the Heart*. He has written for publications such as *Decision, Discipleship Journal, Christian Single, Breakaway, Today's Christian, Light & Life, Sports Spectrum, Sharing the VICTORY*, and many others. He is also a blogger whose work has been nominated for several awards. GPN Mentor of Carolyn Meiller and Lawrence Clark.

Photo by john@johnthurman.net.

Photo by john@johnthurman.net.